JACK RUSSELL TERRIER

Esther Verhoef

JACK RUSSELL TERRIER

REBO
PUBLISHERS

© 2001 Zuid Boekprodukties
© 2006 Rebo Publishers

Text: Esther Verhoef
Photographs: Esther Verhoef/Furry Tails e. a.
Design and layout: Minkowsky Graphics, Enkhuizen, The Netherlands
Reproduction: De ZrIJ, Maarssen, The Netherlands
Pre-press services: Artedit s.r.o., Prague, The Czech Republic
English translation: American Pie, London, UK and Sunnyvale, California

ISBN 13: 978-90-366-1552-5
ISBN 10: 90-366-1552-6

CONTENTS

FOREWORD

In many breeds of dog, the original characteristics required for the work they were bred to do, have mellowed, in the course of time, some more than others. The Jack Russell terrier is an exception. Despite its tremendous popularity with non-hunters, it is still able and more than willing to do the work for which it was originally bred, and do it well. I have written this book for the large group of non-hunting Jack Russell-lovers, but the characteristics and features of this breed are so closely related to its original job of fox-hunting that the book could never be complete without discussing this kind of hunting. Whenever I had the chance to go fox-hunting, I seized the opportunity so that I would be able to grant you a little insight into the Jack Russell terrier's original work, thus helping you appreciate the dog's character, both visible and otherwise.

Circumference

When reaching the spot in the forest where the fox has gone to ground, you will notice just how narrow the entrance is to

The entrance to a fox's den.

a fox's den. The dog can hardly squeeze through it. It suddenly dawns on me why the breed standard requires that the chest of a Jack Russell terrier can be encompassed with two hands. If it were any larger, the dog wouldn't be able to squeeze through the opening or it would become get trapped further along the tunnel. That is why hunters select their working terriers not just for their character but also for their size and circumference. Some of the Jack Russells I have seen at shows would certainly not be able to do that kind of work. They might have the right disposition but they would simply be too big or too broad.

*Right:
This dog is wearing a transmitter so it can be continuously monitored.*

Transmitter

The bitch used for today's hunt has been fitted with a collar containing a transmitter. The owner has a receiver, enabling him to trace the dog constantly. Should she get into any difficulties, the receiver will be able to determine her position and how far inside the tunnel she has penetrated with a fair degree of accuracy, so that she could be dug out. A spade appears to be standard equipment for anyone using Jack Russells for hunting. Nor is a transmitter by any means a superfluous luxury; a fox's den, with its miles of tunnels, can be absolutely huge. This soon becomes apparent when the dog, once unleashed, disappears underground in a flash and the owner, following the transmitter signals above ground, walks the same route as his dog, zigzagging and slaloming for twenty or thirty yards.

Barking

The dog has been underground for a good ten minutes and we can feel the tension rising above ground. Will the den be empty? All we can hear is birdsong and the wind rustling the leaves. But things are not always what seem. One of the hunters puts his ear to the ground near the entrance to the den and beckons to me to come and listen to the sound so familiar to him. Flat on the ground, one ear to the entrance, I can hear a muffled "coughing." It isn't actually a dog choking, but a loudly yapping Jack Russell, barking at a fox under ground, in an attempt to drive it out of its den. The few feet of earth between us and the dog and fox muffle what would otherwise be a shrill yapping. The hunter takes up his position at the exit from the den, as it can't be long now until the fox appears. I feel a tremendous sense of respect for the little dog. She's a good few feet below ground, in a maze of tunnels so narrow that she can't even turn around. She can see nothing at all in the pitch darkness and she is all alone with no backup whatsoever, facing an "enemy" that is much bigger than she is and on home ground to boot. She nevertheless stands there bark-

The dog needs no encouraging to disappear into a fox's den.

ing convincingly and fearlessly. There can be no doubt about it – the dog has plenty of guts.

The fox

The hunter has his gun poised. In a few minutes, the fox bolts out of its den and the hunter hits the target. Seconds later, the Jack Russell wanders out of the tunnel. She's covered in mud and, squinting at the bright light. She shakes herself thoroughly before her owner quickly puts her back on the leash. The transmitter can be removed; she's done her work for the day. She's panting and her little body is trembling but her eyes are shining. Today's exertion is clearly not to be compared with a game of flyball or an agility test.

Inborn

I asked the hunters how these dogs are trained for this work, because no commands are given, everything happens almost "automatically." Apparently most Jack Russells are not actually trained to hunt. They just naturally have what it takes to do so. It is a matter of deselecting when breeding dogs that are too high-spirited or too uncooperative. Later, we discovered that this hunting Jack Russell bitch did not even come from pure hunting lines. Her mother had never even seen a real live fox. Practically every Jack Russell is capable of hunting foxes without training. Some know exactly what they are doing the first time round, others need a few trial runs, but they soon know what to do and instinctively get it right. So to any non-hunting Jack Russell owner who has merely fallen for the little dog's cheerfulness and appeal, be warned – you'll be surprised what the rascal can do, given the chance!

Esther Verhoef

HISTORY

In the beginning....

Great Britain long enjoyed a fox-hunting tradition. Packs of hounds were set on the fox's trail and they would follow its scent, baying loudly. The hunters, usually on horseback, followed the hounds, who captured the fox after a chase, that sometimes lasted for hours. However, the fox often went to ground, hiding in its den so that neither the hounds nor the hunter could reach it. Then a purpose-bred terrier appeared on the scene, and it was set at the entrance to the fox's den. These terriers were full of courage and spirit. They battled their way through to the fox in next to no time, often many feet underground, and just kept barking at the animal until it was final-

Working (Fox) terriers.

ly forced out of the safety of its den. It was important that the fox was not bitten (to death), as this would mean the end of the hunt and that was hardly the object of the exercise.
The terriers used for foxhunting were called "working terriers." The fox terrier also belongs to this category of dogs.

No uniformity

Photos taken of fox terriers in the nineteenth and early twentieth centuries offer an extremely varied impression of the "breed." There was no uniformity of type, the terriers being of many different colors, coat textures, and sizes. That

Right: Two Parsons.

is hardly surprising, considering that hunters chose their dogs for their zest for work and suitability for this specific form of hunting, and soil conditions were not the same everywhere. In the mid-nineteenth century, dog-breeding was booming and non-hunters also became interested in the fox terrier. Breeders were barely interested in the dogs' hunting capacities but concentrated on their appearance. Fox terriers entered the show ring, where the emphasis lay on good looks. A breed standard was drawn up, and the dogs that were selected had to be more refined and of a more uniform type. This eventually led to the "handsome" fox terrier we know today.

Parson John Russell

Many hunters were saddened to see the "loss" of their working terriers. The new terriers were too big for underground work and the character they needed for hunting was also starting to mellow. The hunters more or less distanced themselves from these show-dogs and continued to breed animals suitable for hunting – often without a pedigree. One such breeder was the man who greatly influenced the development of the (Parson) Jack Russell terrier, the English clergyman, Jack Russell. This controversial parson lived from 1795 through 1883. He was very keen on using terriers to hunt foxes and badgers, and over the years bred many litters of dogs that, in his opinion, had both the right character and the right appearance. Most of the dogs he bred ended up belonging to hunters and thanks to their outstanding working abilities the name of John Russell soon became a household name in the English hunting world.

A Jack Russell terrier bareback riding.

Normal leg versus short leg

Every so often, a strain of suitable short-legged terriers were added to the breed. Short-legged pups with the right hunting abilities went to hunters who found that there were both advantages and disadvantages to their short legs. One disadvantage was that the dogs had trouble keeping up with the pack of hounds, so they had to be carried on horseback and only released if a fox had taken cover in its den. The advantage of its modest size then became immediately obvious; under certain circumstances these dogs were often better able than their counterparts with normal length legs at penetrating deep into a den. Short-legged terriers were sometimes considered unfit for hunting purposes, however, and were sold to non-hunters. Many went to farmers and horse-owners, who valued the dogs for the way they managed to keep the stables and yard free of vermin. Their qualities as a companion did not go unnoticed either. In the end, the short-legged Jack Russells attained international fame sooner than the Parsons, their relatives with longer legs.

Parson John Russell (illustration by N.H.J. Baird, 1902).

Recognition

While the breed can boast a fairly impressive history, it was a long time before the Kennel Club accepted them. That is hardly surprising, as breeders of the (Parson) Jack Russell had been against official recognition of the breed from the start, because recognition would mean that the dogs would end up in the show circuit. For many working breeds, pedigree status was inseparable from an aspiration to refine their appearance, and this resulted in concessions in terms of the dogs' original working aptitude and abilities. Lovers of the working (Parson) Jack Russell terrier found this unacceptable, however.

On July 2, 1990 the Parson Jack Russell terrier was finally granted provisional recognition as a breed by the F.C.I (Fédération Cynologique Internationale). This meant that the breeder unions and associations of the around 60 countries belonging to the F.C.I. officially recognize pedigrees for the breed and Jack Russells are now welcome at shows and able to compete for the championship. The Jack Russell terrier has not yet been fully recognized by the F.C.I., but its member

Two Jack Russells and a Parson.

There are many similarities between the "original" type of fox terrier and the Parson Jack Russell.

Right:
A faithful vermin
exterminator on
farms.

organizations in Australia, New Zealand, The Netherlands, Ireland, Japan, and South Africa recognize it as a breed. In these countries, the dogs are temporarily judged on the basis of the Australian breed standard. Considering the near worldwide popularity of the compact Jack Russell terrier, other countries are expected to follow suit soon, as will the F.C.I.

The differences
There are various differences between the Parson Jack Russell and the true Jack Russell. The most obvious difference is the size; the Jack Russell terrier is a shorter than the Parson, due to its shorter legs, and heavier for its build. There are also differences between the two breed standards in chest width and how the ears are carried. A white dog with markings on the head and root of the tail is preferred for both breeds, although these markings are only specifically referred to in the breed standard for the Parson Jack Russell. In all other aspects, including character, the breed standards are largely the same.

2 BREED STANDARDS

2.1 Breed standard for the Parson Jack Russell terrier

General
Sturdy, tenacious, working terrier with an aptitude for working underground. Alert, active, and agile, built for speed and endurance.

Head
The skull should be flat, moderately broad, gradually narrowing to the eyes. The stop should be short. The length from nose to stop should be slightly shorter than from the stop to occiput. The jaws should be strong and muscular. Teeth should have a perfect, regular, and complete scissor bite, i.e. upper teeth closely overlapping lower teeth and set square to the jaws. The eyes should be almond-shaped, fairly deep-set, and dark, with a keen expression. The ears should be small, vee-shaped, dropping forward, and carried close to the head. There should be no on the top of the skull. The nose should be black.

Body
Well-balanced. The neck should be clean muscular, of reasonable length, gradually widening to the shoulders. The length of the back from the withers to the root of the tail should be the same as the height, measured from the withers to the ground (the dog should be longer than its height). The back should be strong and straight. The loins should be slightly arched. The chest should be of moderate depth, capable of being spanned behind the shoulders by average-size hands. The tail should be strong, straight, and set fairly high. It is customarily docked to a length proportionate to the body, providing a good handhold. The front legs should be strong and straight, with joints turning neither inward nor outward. The shoulders should be long and sloping, well laid back, and cleanly cut at the withers. The elbows should be close to the body, working free of the sides. The hindquarters should be strong and muscular with good angulation and bend of stifle, the hocks set low, and the rear pasterns parallel, so they are able to provide plenty of propulsion.
The feet should be compact with firm pads,

Smooth-haired
Parson Jack
Russell terrier.

turning neither inward nor outward. The gait should be free, lively, and well-coordinated, with parallel movements when viewed from in front and behind. The skin should be thick and loose.

Height
The ideal height at the withers for dogs is 14 inches and for bitches 13 inches. For an indefinite period, the height for dogs and bitches should be no less than 10½ inches. Dogs are not considered untrue to the breed if they are not the ideal height, however, and such dogs may breed without restriction.

Coat and color
The coat should be naturally wiry, close, and dense, whether smooth, broken, or rough. The belly and undersides should be hairy. Color: entirely white or predominantly white with tan, lemon, or black markings, preferably confined to the head and/or root of the tail.

Temperament
A working terrier with the aptitude and build to go to ground after the fox and run with the hounds. Bold and friendly.

2.2 Breed standard for the Jack Russell terrier

General
The Jack Russell terrier is a strong, active, agile, clever working terrier with a brave character and flexible body of medium length. Its sprightly gait matches its keen expression. Tail-docking is optional. The coat may be smooth, broken, or rough.

Head
The skull should be flat and of moderate width, gradually narrowing to the eyes, and on to a firm muzzle with very strong jaws. The stop should be well defined but not overpronounced. The length from the stop to the nose should be slightly shorter than from the stop to the occiput, and the jaw muscles should be well developed. The nose should be black. The well-developed, powerful jaws should have tight-fitting, pigmented lips and a scissor bite with strong teeth. Button or dropped ear-flaps, strong and extremely mobile. The eyes should be small and dark, their expression alert. They should not be protruding and the eyelids should fit closely. The eye-rims should be black.

Body
The neck should be strong and clean, allowing the head to be carried with poise. The chest should be deep rather than wide,

with good clearance from the ground, the brisket located at a point midway between the ground and the withers.

The body should be marginally longer than it is tall, measuring slightly longer from the withers to the root of tail than from the withers to the ground. The back should be straight. The ribs should be well-rounded, flattening at the sides, so that two hands can span the girth behind the elbows – 15–17 inches. The loins should be short, strong, and muscular. The shoulders should slope well back and not be too muscular. The forelegs should be straight from shoulder to toe, viewed from either the front or the side, and with sufficient length in the upper arm to ensure that the elbows are set under the body. The sternum should be clearly visible. The hindquarters should be strong and muscular, and balanced in proportion to the shoulders. Viewed from behind, while in a free-standing position, the hind legs should be parallel. The stifles should be clearly angular and hocks set low. The feet should be rounded, hard, and with firm pads, not large, with toes moderately arched, turning neither inward nor outward. The gait should be true, free, and springy. The tail should droop when at rest. When wagging, it should be erect and if it has been docked, the tip should be at the same level as the ears.

Left:
Jack Russell terrier, smooth-haired bitch.

Right:
Jack Russell terrier, rough-haired dog.

Size
Ideally the terrier should be 10–12 inches high, weighing approximately a pound an inch of shoulder height. So a 10-inch dog should weigh around 10 pounds and a 12-inch dog should weigh around 12 pounds.

Coat and color
The coat may be smooth, broken, or rough. The coat must be weatherproof. White must predominate, with black, tan, or brown markings.

Temperament
Bold and fearless, friendly and confident.

3 THE PARSON AND THE JACK RUSSELL IN CLOSEUP

Working dogs

Parsons are working dogs, seldom seen in the show-ring.

Jack Russell terriers used to be working dogs, as indeed most breeds were. But unlike most other breeds, the Jack Russell terrier of today is still very similar to the original. From day one, breeders aspired to maintain the hunting abilities of the breed. Appearance was of secondary importance, that is to say, the dog had to have the best build and character for the type of work it was required to do. Although neither breed is much used for hunting these days, many breeders still adhere to the original breeding objectives. They are averse to far-reaching refinement of the appearance that – as in so many other breeds – has often come at the expense of reduced working ability. For this reason, neither the Jack Russell nor the Parson are often seen at dog shows. They are unsophisticated and that is exactly what so many people find attractive about

Good socialization skills are essential.

them. The breed has hardly any breed-related, genetic abnormalities and a life expectancy of around fifteen years is certainly not over-optimistic. All this means that these terriers have retained their original characteristics without any signs of degeneracy.

This dog is no lazybones!
Jack Russell terriers are intelligent working dogs and simply bursting with energy. A Jack Russell terrier is particularly useful on a farm or in stables, where it tracks and eliminates vermin, and announces any visitors. If allowed to hunt, it will have ample opportunity to prove its talents and to expend all that energy, but in the average family home, even in the country, there is usually not enough adventure for such a spirited, energetic, and impetuous little dog. So it is up to the owner to give the dog plenty of things to do. Don't expect the dog to adapt to a placid lifestyle; it's just not going to happen. In view of its character, chances are that it will go looking for all kinds of mischief that neither its owner nor the neighbors will appreciate. Both breeds are therefore only suitable for people who like to do things with their dog. These terriers are not inclined to waste their days away in utter contentment in front of an open fire.

How do they get along with other animals?

Whether or not your Jack Russell terrier behaves well with other pets, such as cats, will largely depend on how well it has been socialized. It has been bred to hunt foxes (as well as badgers and rabbits) and therefore has a fair dose of hunting instinct. If you don't have any other pets yourself, it is important to regularly let your pup come into contact with friendly cats, rabbits, and other small animals. If a young puppy's new home is already home to other pets, it will normally have no problem in accepting its new housemates. Once it has grown up with parrots, ferrets, and cats, a Jack Russell would not harm a hair (or a feather) of their heads. They could even become friends. The opposite is also true, however. If you are considering adopting an older dog that has had little contact with other pets, or one that has been used for hunting, you should be aware that it will consider any other pets as prey and will act accordingly. A period of socialization, used to good effect, makes a world of difference, but remember, your dog is still a feisty hunting dog that once outdoors, will chase after

Their aggression toward other dogs can be tempered by being raised correctly and through socialization.

any animal on the run, whether in the country or in a residential area. Having said that, living together in harmony with very small pets, such as hamsters and rats, really would be asking too much of most Jack Russells.

Other dogs

Inherent to the feisty terrier character, Jack Russells can behave quite fiercely toward other dogs and will seldom avoid a challenge. The size of their opponent does not deter them one bit and considering their undaunted courage, things could obviously go very wrong if they come up against a big, strong adversary. There is really nothing amusing about a little puppy excitedly yapping or letting fly at another one of its own kind passing by. So you should never allow your dog to bark at other dogs or, worse still, attack them. Socialize it with friendly, stable dogs and prevent it being allowed to engage in this kind of behavior from an early age. If your puppy is to grow into a dog that, while it won't be bullied, still behaves normally toward other dogs without getting too unsettled when challenged, this is largely up to you. If you already have a bitch, you'd do best to choose a dog as a new companion, and vice versa. Opposite sexes tend to get on very well together, while two bitches or two dogs can become difficult.

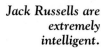

Jack Russells are extremely intelligent.

Man's best friend

Jack Russell terriers truly are man's best friend. They bark when any visitors arrive, but that is all. Your visitors will usually be welcomed with great enthusiasm, on the principle of "the more the merrier." They are not one-man dogs and by no means shy. A well-socialized Jack Russell can also be exceptionally good with children, your own children and other people's children alike. Jack Russells are not "soft", however. They have a sporting nature and are always ready for a game or a bit of fun. It can't be too boisterous for them and it never lasts long enough. They certainly owe a lot of their popularity to their good-natured behavior with children and their sporting disposition. However, a Jack Russell terrier is not a toy and children must be taught that a dog is a living creature that should be respected. Even a hardened Jack Russell terrier can suddenly decide that enough is enough.

Independent or (dis)obedient?
Jack Russell terriers have always been working dogs. Countless decisions when the dog is confronted with the outside of a fox's den or finds itself inside the den are not prompted by the owner, but taken by the dog itself.

Bye boss, I'm just popping underground for a minute!

... mice? It is because these dogs are so dependent on their own strength and judgment that they need a consistent upbringing by a decisive owner. They do not obey their owner because they want to please him or her; they only ever do anything to please themselves – out of pure selfishness. So keep the exercises as fun and challenging as possible. A Jack Russell terrier detests being bored so if the exercises are too unchallenging and repetitive, it will become decidedly uncooperative. If a Jack Russell refuses to obey a command, that actually says more about the owner than the dog itself. The owner is not doing the exercises in a way that will appeal to the dog. Many owners cannot (or will not) see through the disarming diversionary tactics of their extremely intelligent little dogs. Overly tolerant or "democratic" owners will find they get more than they bargained for with this breed. The dog simply does what it feels like doing.

Not the stay-at-home type

Jack Russells are not what you might call the stay-at-home type. If they pick up an interesting scent, they'll want to know more. In a residential area, the scent of a bitch in heat can be reason enough for a dog to dig his way out under the fence, and to an unleashed terrier out in the woods, the scent of game, or the inviting entrance to a rabbit burrow, or a fox's den irresistible. It is therefore important that you fence your yard or garden well and keep a close eye on your unleashed dog when out walking. Of course, some states have a leash law and insist you keep your dog on a leash in the city. This is particularly advisable with a Jack Russell, no matter how hard you have tried to socialize it.

If a Jack Russell has plenty to do, it will be less inclined to go searching for fun elsewhere because it's bored. In the woods, for example, the owner with an intriguing-looking ball in his/her hand could be far more interesting than a rabbit. If an owner has insight into the dog's way of thinking, and is prepared to take the time and effort, he/she will have little trouble with the "disobedience" so typical of many terriers, because the dog will have discovered that having the master around him is much more fun than "doing its own thing."

In brief

Whether your Jack Russell terrier becomes the cute, cheerful, uncomplicated, sporting dog that everybody envies, or the proverbial Jack Russell "terror," is very much up to you. Upbringing and socialization make a world of difference with this breed, but that doesn't mean that the owner can sit back and relax after that. It would be impossible to deal with every aspect of dog behavior and upbringing here, so before you bring your puppy home, read several good books that deal with this subject in depth. It is also advisable to follow good obedience classes with your puppy. Remember that your dog could live to age 15 or older. If you invest in it properly now, you will both have many years of fun ahead of you.

Characteristics in a nutshell:

- (Very) active and energetic
- Indefatigable
- Extremely intelligent
- Enterprising
- Courageous
- Independent
- Sporting

- Alert
- Playful
- Uncomplicated
- Watchful, but not shy
- Strong hunting instinct

4 BUYING A PUPPY

Dog or bitch?

One of the first choices you will have to make if you want to buy a Jack Russell is the sex. Most people simply "prefer" either dogs or bitches, which makes the choice a very personal one, but there are also practical differences between the two sexes. Bitches only urinate when they have to and squat to do so. Dogs don't just urinate, they frequently scent-mark, lifting their leg at things. Bitches are in season for about three weeks, twice a year, during which time they are fertile and will attract dogs. This puts off a lot of people, but spaying or a contraceptive injection can stop the seasons, either temporarily or permanently. Consider that bitches only contemplate reproduction twice a year, whereas dogs offer their service all year round. The scent of a bitch in season somewhere in the neighborhood can unsettle a dog so much that he hardly eats for days or even takes to his heels to go searching for the female in question.

There are minor differences in character. Male dogs are often more stable, because they are not subject to hormonal changes, and they are slightly more independent. There are physical differences too, of course, although these are not as pronounced as in many other breeds. The dogs are usually a little larger and sturdier than bitches. If you already have a bitch, no matter what the breed, you should buy a dog. Dog-bitch combinations usually cause no problems but two or more dogs or bitches can be intolerant of one another.

Dogs urinate more frequently than bitches.

Where to look for your terrier

Jack Russell terriers are immensely popular and, as always, this attracts "breeders" trying to jump on the financial bandwaggon. An awful lot of "Jack Russell terriers" are bred without a pedigree, although this seldom happens with Parsons. Usually the dog you would be getting is not a Jack Russell terriers at all but a crossbred fox terrier or some other cross that vaguely resembles a Jack Russell. In terms of both appearance and character, these look-alikes can be very different from what you would expect of a purebred Jack Russell terrier. Abnormal behavior is often seen in pups that are not purebred, for example. Purebred Jack Russells are usually healthy dogs that can live to quite a ripe old age. The influence of other breeds in puppies that are not purebred, on the other hand, may cause genetic diseases or deformities. Legally speaking, you wouldn't have a leg to stand on if you buy a dog without a pedigree that suffers from a (genetic) disease. Obviously, the "breeder" of such pups will do his utmost to convince you that a pedigree would only make them unnecessarily expensive. Don't fall for that old trick! Only if you buy a Jack Russell terrier with an official pedigree, can you be sure that the dog truly is purebred and will therefore have the character and appearance typical of the breed and the good health that comes with it.

Good wine needs no bush
There are several things to look out for as far as the breeder is concerned. For one thing, remember the old saying, "good wine needs no bush." Of course a breeder is going to praise his or her dogs, but the average reliable breeder will be far more

A Jack Russell-Beagle cross. Hard to distinguish from the "real thing" as a puppy!

Kennel dogs can make wonderful family pets, provided the breeder takes his or her responsibility seriously.

interested in what you have to offer his or her carefully bred pup than in a swift sale. Don't be blinded by the term "champion stock." In reality, practically all puppies, whatever the breed, will have one or more champions among their ancestry. It only needs a single champion in the pedigree for it to be called "champion stock," so there is nothing special about that. Finally, even if both parents prove to be top dogs, that says nothing at all about the quality of the puppies. Top dogs when bred can produce run-of-the-mill puppies and alternatively, with a stroke of luck, the opposite can happen. The breeder can never guarantee that the pup you buy will eventually become a show champion. At best, based on years of experience, you could cherish high hopes.

Hygiene, space and socialization

Observe the environment the pups are living in. It is important for young puppies to become acquainted with everyday sights and sounds like the noise of the vacuum cleaner and the television. They should expect to be stroked and petted regularly, and cuddled by lots of different people, preferably including children, so that they learn that people won't hurt them. A puppy that has not been familiarized with these kinds of things at an early age has really missed out on a vital part of its upbringing, and unfortunately this cannot be made up for later. The chance of such a puppy growing into an erratic, nervous dog is very real. Good impressions at an early age are therefore vital. Puppies reared in the home will automatically gain enough experience, but kennel pups must be allowed into the home for at least a quarter of an hour a day to socialize. A good breeder knows this and will take his or her responsibility seriously. "Breeders" that have hardly socialized their puppies at all have devised a trick to help them sell the pups anyway. It is this. You won't be allowed to see the whole litter, the "breeder" will just drop one or two puppies into your lap. A scared little puppy will have no escape so it will just stay there, petrified. This endears most people and the sale is as good as guaranteed. Don't fall for this old trick, which unfortunately is still employed frequently by irresponsible dog breeders.

It is perfectly normal for you to be allowed to see where the pups live with their mother so that you can see where they all live and they are free to come up to meet you. The breeder should only be a little cautious if the pups have not yet been inoculated. He or she obviously doesn't know where you've been before coming to see him or her and you might unintentionally infect the pups. The place in which the puppies are kept should be hygienic and spacious. Pups growing up in too small area, especially one that is not cleaned often enough, become accustomed to the continuous presence of urine and feces. They sleep next to them and have no choice but to walk in them. These pups will be very hard to house-train later.

If the pups have not yet been inoculated, you might not be allowed to touch them (yet).

Impression of the dam, the breeder and the puppies
If you go to see a litter, watch how the breeder treats the puppies and the dam. This will tell you a lot. Also observe the

The mother is her puppies' prime role model.

mother's character and behavior. Prompted by her hormones, she will be especially protective of her pups. After all you are a complete stranger to her, so it is quite normal for her to be a little aloof at first, although that need not necessarily be the case. But it is not a good sign if she is clearly mistrustful, barking non-stop or demonstrating anxious or nervous behavior. Even if her unstable behavior is not hereditary, she is not setting a good example for her offspring. Her pups see their mother as their role model. The character of the sire is also important as far as heredity is concerned, but as not all breeders have a sire themselves, you will often only be shown a photograph of the father. In the case of a reliable breeder you can take him or her at his word but unless the dog lives out of state, there is nothing to stop you visiting the owner of the sire.

Watch how the puppies themselves behave. If they are not asleep they will usually be only too happy to come straight over to meet you. Healthy puppies are playful and enterprising with an open character. They see your presence as an adventure. Puppies that recoil, or that are shy or indifferent, are therefore best left with the breeder.

Jack Russells can live to a fair old age, so a prospective owner should think carefully before buying one.

Finally, observe the puppies' appearance. Swollen bellies are quite normal if they've only just eaten, but can also be symptomatic of a worm infection. Other signs that should set you thinking are fleas (or flea dirt) in the coat, traces of diarrhea, runny eyes or nose, dirty ears, and a scruffy, dirty coat.

Which puppy?

One of the most persistent old wives' tales is that you should choose the pup that approaches you first. Although dogs have their preferences too, young puppies that are physically and mentally healthy will almost always come up to you to size up the situation. The first one to bite in your shoe is usually the cheekiest, most dominant one of the litter. This is a pup that will demand more insight and authority from you during its upbringing. If you are actually looking for a feisty little dog, then this could well be the perfect choice, but most families would benefit more from a puppy whose character is a little more average. In practically every litter, there is also a puppy that is a little shyer than the rest. They will flourish in a quiet environment but seldom come into their own in a bustling household. If in doubt, always ask the breeder's advice. You can only see the pups very briefly, whereas he or she is with them every day. In most cases, the breeder will be the best person to assess which pup would suit for your home situation best.

Which puppy?

5 A PUPPY IN THE HOME

What have I been given?

When you go to fetch your puppy, most breeders will give you some food for the first few days and possibly a booklet or brochure with useful tips on raising the pup and other information the breeder considers important. Almost all breeders will give you a diet sheet. This will tell you the sort of food you can best feed your puppy in the coming months, the quantities and how many times a day it should be fed. It is advisable to follow these instructions from the outset, because any change in food could cause diarrhea and your puppy will already have enough changes to cope with. It is also a good idea to ask for a piece of the blanket from the whelping-box. At home, you can put this in the crate or basket so that your puppy will have a familiar scent with it. Something you should always be given is the inoculation certificate, stating when and against what your puppy has been inoculated and when these inoculations should be repeated.

*Jack Russell
puppy.*

You will often be asked to sign a contract of sale that specifies the rights and obligations of both seller and buyer. Ensure that the content is reasonable before signing. A breeder will usually not be able to give you a pedigree immediately because the paperwork takes time and by the time it arrives, the puppies will be registered in the name of their new owners. The pedigree will be sent to you later, although some breeders like to deliver it to you personally. If you buy a puppy from someone who is not a member of the breeders' association, make sure that it has its computer chip inserted before you take it home. Contrary to what you may be told, a pup that has not had the chip inserted has not been registered, and so will never be given a pedigree.

Taking your puppy home

If you go to fetch your puppy by car, and the journey takes longer than half an hour, stop on the way to give the puppy a chance to relieve itself – but keep it on the leash! Many young dogs get travel sick so it's a good idea to have a towel or suchlike at hand. Once you are home, before going inside, give the puppy another chance to go to the toilet, preferably in the place you plan to do this for the next few weeks. Once indoors, let the puppy rest as much as possible. It has so many new impressions to cope with and it can do that best while resting. Show it the water-bowl so that it knows where to find it. If the breeder gave you a piece of blanket from the whelping-box, put this in its crate or basket. It will be exhausted from the adventure, and if attracted by a familiar scent, it will snuggle up quietly in bed.

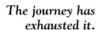

The journey has exhausted it.

Children and their new housemate

If you have children, you are going to have to pull out all the stops to prevent them from dragging the puppy around everywhere, calling it all the time or giving it tidbits. Teach your children that they must not disturb the dog while it is sleeping, or when it's taken itself off to its crate or basket. Not while it's still a little puppy, and not even later when it's a fully grown dog. Puppies that are continually disturbed in their sleep, or that get dragged about can become decidedly neurotic.

The first night

The first night is not pleasant experience for dog-owners. The pup is usually completely alone for the first time, without its brothers and sisters and without his mother. A lonely puppy looking for contact will start to bark, whine, and howl. This is a natural reaction and is best ignored. That is because if your puppy gets a reaction to its "wake-up call" it will make a habit of making itself heard whenever it doesn't want to be alone, and not only at night but even when you've just gone out to the market for a few minutes. And it will continue with this behavior for the rest of its life. It is better to ignore your puppy entirely, however hard that might be. So don't call to it from your bed, or go and scold or comfort it. Initially, it won't make the slightest bit of difference to him whether you are angry with it or not. The main thing is that calling has had an effect, it produced some kind of response. It often helps to wrap the blanket from the whelping-box around a hot water bottle. The combination of warmth and familiar scents will soon send your puppy to sleep.

6 WHAT YOU WILL NEED

Baskets and crates or cages

The basket

Parson and Jack Russell terriers are enterprising little dogs that really like getting their teeth into things. If you take this into account when choosing a basket, you will almost always decide on a hard plastic bed or, better still, a crate or cage. Soft baskets and the specially designed doggy beanbag pillows might look very comfortable and be much more attractive, but for the average terrier they form the ideal chewing material. Once your Jack Russell terrier has learned how much fun it can be to chew its bed it is difficult, if not impossible, to break it of the habit later. You can lay a blanket in the basket or crate. Give it a good shake every day and wash it regularly. Buy more than one blanket if you can, so that you are never stuck

Plastic beds can also be subjected to a durability test.

Luxurious basket.

Doggy beanbag pillow.

without one if the other is in the wash. It is worth remembering that woolen blankets are not very practical, because dog hairs get caught in the weave and wool is difficult to wash. You would be better off buying a smoother type of blanket that is easier to wash and dries more quickly, one which is less likely to get matted with dog hairs.

Crate or cage
A crate or cage is a much better investment than a basket. Crates and cages have the added advantage that they can be closed, which is perfect for house-breaking and for that "destructive" period every pup goes through. There are other advantages too. A lightweight crate or cage can be used inside the car for extra safety, and a puppy in a crate cannot chew (poisonous) plants or electricity cables, either. If there are children in the house, it will be impossible to be watchful at all times, especially when friends come to play. A crate can then prove ideal.

Some people think a crate or cage is "cruel" but, provided you don't use it as a punishment, the opposite is true. A dog that chews things to bits during your absence or wets and messes the house, has an angry, moaning owner to answer to, while a "crate puppy" cannot do a thing wrong so it is always a "Good Boy!"

Crates are strongly built and your puppy will not be able to chew them to bits, the way it would a basket. A good quality crate is not cheap, but it will last a dog's lifetime and by using one you can avoid much more expensive damage to your furniture and household goods. However, it is not a dog-cage. It is intended as means of shutting your puppy or mature dog away safely for a short while, if you are unable to watch over it and it can also spend the nights there. A puppy should always be introduced to a crate in a positive way. Don't force anything on it. To make the crate attractive, you could put its blanket in there, as well as some playthings, and something to chew on that the puppy is only given when it is in the crate. Given the right introduction, your puppy will go to the crate of its own accord whenever it wants to rest or sleep.

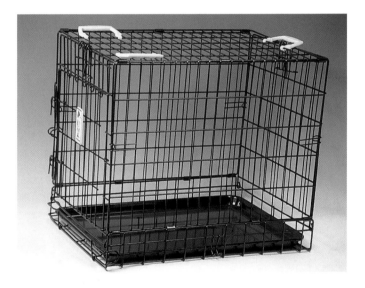

Wire crate.

This type of crate offers the same protection as a "wolf's den."

Soft nylon collar.

Collars and leashes

There is a difference between the collar you would buy for a young puppy and the one used for a mature dog. People often buy their puppies a collar to "grow into." This is not a good idea because a puppy could slip out of an ill-fitting collar, the consequences of which could be disastrous, particularly near a busy road. Too big a collar isn't very comfortable either, so you'd do better to buy one that fits properly.

There is a very wide variety of collars available today. A nylon collar is ideal for a puppy. The material is practically indestructible, easy to wash, lightweight, and comfortable. You could buy a leather one later, but be sure that the inside is lined with softer leather or material. A suitable leash would be 4 to 5 feet long, supple, and lightweight. Nylon is more durable than poor quality leather and therefore preferable. You could also buy a retractable leash, which would enable you to give your terrier more freedom when you take it out.

Food and water bowls

Food and water bowls are available in all shapes and sizes. Choose a food bowl that is large, to prevent your puppy spilling its food. There are many different types, varying from stainless steel to durable plastic, lightweight plastic, and earthenware. The advantage of the lightweight plastic bowls is that they are inexpensive, but they tend to slide across the floor and can easily get knocked over. Furthermore, the plastic gets scratched quite quickly, so that after a while the bowl is not only quite awful to look at but it is also hard to clean. Another disadvantage of lightweight bowls is that your puppy might discover how much fun it is to run around with it in his mouth. These disadvantages do not apply to the same degree to the heavier quality plastics. Glazed earthenware bowls are quite heavy and easy to clean, but an obvious disadvantage is that they are breakable.

Stainless steel bowls are simple to clean and practically indestructible. However, they do tend to slide across the floor, so
you would also need a special holder or mat, although some
stainless steel bowls currently on the market already have a
non-slip underside.

*Stainless steel
food bowls with
stand.*

Chews and treats

Chews are often considered a "treat" for a dog but should, in
fact, be part of the standard diet for both puppies and mature
dogs. To start with, they will relieve boredom, so that your terrier will be less inclined to dig his teeth into your furniture or
other worldly goods. Chewing on something tough will also

*There are all
kinds of chews.*

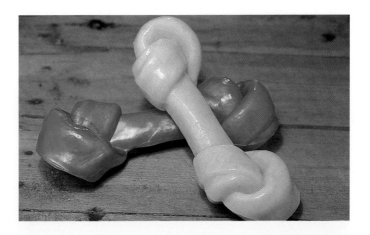

Nylon chews are safe.

Floss ropes; fun but only under supervision.

help keep his teeth clean, avoiding plaque and other dental problems. There is a host of chewing toys and treats on the market but not all of them serve equally well as a toothbrush or occupational therapy. Chew-sticks and strips might well be delicious but your average Jack Russell terrier will devour one within seconds. Pressed rawhide bones are much better, or

boiled veal bones or beef bones. Synthetic bones, made of meat trimmings are a safe and durable alternative to these chews. The effect is just the same as that of traditional chews but they are more hygienic and they last longer. You can read more about things to chew in the chapter on feeding.

Durable toys.

Toys

The range of toys on sale for dogs is simply vast, ranging from floss ropes to soft balls and little latex doggies. Be critical in your choice of a toy and try to look at it through your dog's eyes. Not every toy is safe for every dog, and every toy has the potential to be dangerous, especially in the case of terriers, who love to bite and chew their playthings. Toys that can be damaged – and that applies to practically all kinds of toys – should only be played with under supervision. That way you can avoid your dog swallowing bits of plastic and suchlike or a toy endangering your dog's health or even life in any other way.

*Right:
Every dog is
naturally
continent.*

7 HOUSE-TRAINING

Every dog is house-trained

In principle, every dog is naturally house-trained. There is not
a single healthy dog that likes to sleep, play, eat, and answer
the call of nature all in the same place. This natural cleanli-
ness can be seen in young puppies while they are still in the
nest. As soon as their mother no longer cleans up their puddles and mess, the pups will try to get as far away as possible
from the nest before relieving themselves. It is important that
they get the chance to do so. The breeder should ensure that
there is enough space and the area in which the pups are kept
should be cleaned thoroughly several times a day. It happens
on rare occasions that a "breeder" gives the puppies too little
space and only cleans up with a cat's lick and a promise. These
pups then have no other choice but to relieve themselves in
their whelping-box and the habit that then forms can result in
them still thinking it quite normal to mess their bed later in
life. This can lead their new owners to despair, because they
are almost incapable of learning the rules of normal house-
training. If you acquire your pup through a responsible breeder, then you will have won half the house-training battle.

Toilet area
When you get your puppy home, it should already be more or
less house-trained. All you have to teach it is that it must consider not only his bed, usually the crate or basket, as its "nest"
but the rest of the house as well. You can start house-training

*When your puppy
puddles outside
it's always a
"good boy!"*

from day one. Choose an outdoor toilet area that is readily accessible and where your puppy will be allowed to relieve itself throughout the entire period of house-training. This will usually be in your own garden or yard or a patch of grass near your home. Remember that the puppy's inoculations will only partially protect your dog against disease. It will still be susceptible to germs, which can also be found in other dogs' feces. So it is vital that you avoid "breeding grounds," such as much used dog toilet areas, until you puppy has had all of its vaccinations. This will usually be at the age of around twelve to fourteen weeks.

Recognizing smells

When house-training, take advantage of the fact that dogs are animals of habit with an excellent sense of smell. A dog will be able to recognize the smell of a previous puddle or mess for a long time. This familiar smell will encourage it to give a repeat performance in the same place. This means that house-training will be much more successful if your dog is allowed to relieve itself in the same place each time. But beware, the same principle also applies indoors! Your Jack Russell terrier is

Dogs can easily smell the puddles they made before.

capable of recognizing its own scent, no matter how many cleaning agents you have used since, and giving a repeat performance. Accidents indoors should therefore be avoided as much as possible, so keep a close eye on your puppy, particularly in the first few weeks. Puppies will usually relieve themselves shortly after eating and soon after waking, but it can't do any harm to initially take it outside every hour. If you see your pup sniffing about and turning round and round, pick it up immediately and put it outside in its toilet area. Don't call it outside, as chances are it'll have an accident en route.

Nighttime

The nights are often the hardest, from a house-training point of view. Your puppy is used to frequently having the chance to go to the toilet outside, but at night it's a different story altogether. The best thing to do is to put your puppy into the crate for the night. To improve the chance of success, make sure that it starts the night with as empty a digestive system as possible and take away the food and water bowls. Before you go to bed – as late as possible, preferably – let your puppy out and make sure that it does actually do something. First thing in the morning, be there in a flash to let it out again. It might even be a good idea to set an alarm clock for the first couple of weeks, to let the puppy out halfway through the night.

> Do not praise your puppy while it's still sniffing around and thinking about doing something, praise it when it has actually finished puddling or messing.

Punishment?

It is understandable that you will feel like punishing your puppy when it keeps having mishaps indoors. However, that is exactly what you shouldn't do, for various reasons. If you catch it in the act and punish it for what he's doing, it might get the idea that you don't want it to relieve itself within your sight. Your puppy will then do its utmost to prevent that from happening again. While you are out walking it will do absolutely nothing but once home, it will go looking for a spot out of your sight. Once a dog demonstrates this kind of behavior, it can be hard to convince it to do otherwise. Neither is it a good idea to punish a puppy for an accident that happened a little earlier. Dogs will link the punishment to what they are doing when

Make sure your dog knows you're pleased with it.

they are punished. So if you punish your puppy for an "old" puddle or pile of mess, then in its eyes you will be scolding it for no reason at all, because it's busy doing something else now. The "guilty" look your puppy adopts while you are raving at him is in fact nothing less than fear of you, its unpredictable pack leader that it just cannot comprehend. So never punish your pup while house-training. The easiest way to house-train your puppy is to avoid accidents wherever possible, give it ample opportunity to get it right and reward it cheerfully when it does get it right. Should your puppy have an accident indoors, say nothing at all, but simply pick it up and put it outside. If it continues doing its business outside, then obviously you should praise it. If you are unable to keep an eye on it, use the crate.

Emotions

There are several kinds of "incontinence," such as submissive urination, that actually have nothing to do with house-training at all. This is when a puppy becomes extremely submissive by rolling on its back, looking away, its tail between its legs, and urinating. This is the most extreme way a dog has of showing you that it considers itself to be of the lowest possible rank. Submissive urination occurs more in puppies than in mature dogs because puppies are often more insecure about their place in the pack.

Dogs that are insecure by nature, can often show this behavior, particularly when confronted with their (dominant) pack leader. When they are being punished, for example or when, in their eyes, you behave in an especially domineering way. This has nothing whatsoever to do with incontinence and should never be punished. On the contrary, a relaxed approach

will often help to improve a situation in which a dog views your leadership as threatening. Another emotion that is often paired with involuntary urination or bowel movement is "excitement urination." Your puppy is so pleased when you come home or stroke it, that it loses all control over its bladder. Again, this has nothing to do with incontinence; your dog will hardly notice what is happening and so cannot prevent it. Most dogs will grow out of it in time. Meanwhile, you can limit the damage in the home by more-or-less ignoring your dog when you get home, first taking it out into the garden and then making a big fuss of it.

Relief on command

It is possible to teach your dog to relieve itself on command. This can be very handy, especially if you live in a busy residential area and there is a dog toilet area nearby that you are obliged to have your dog use.

In practice, this entails you first taking your dog to a toilet area and giving it an opportunity to relieve itself, which then enables you to take it for a nice long walk without causing a nuisance to anyone else. You can teach your dog to do this on command by linking a particular word to the deed, "puddle" for instance. Whenever your puppy puddles or messes of its own accord, you cheerfully say "puddle, good boy!"regardless of where outside it has been to the toilet. An intelligent dog

---

Young puppies will not have full control of their bladder until they are about 5 or 6 months old, so until then "accidents" will happen.

An embarrassing situation that could be avoided by teaching the dog to relieve itself on command.

will soon connect the word "puddle" with actual urination and on hearing that word will also hear nature calling. Then all you need to do is to say the word at the place where the dog is allowed to relieve itself, e.g. a toilet area. Don't forget to reward your dog if it actually does anything.

You can fence off a corner of the garden or yard for the dog to use as a toilet.

Sudden incontinence in a dog that has been fully continent for some time could be symptomatic of a health problem such as diabetes, cystitis, or even kidney failure. Have your dog checked by a veterinarian before jumping to conclusions.

8 RANK

Pack behavior

Just like their wild ancestors, dogs are pack animals. Packs are governed by a strict hierarchy, at the head of which an alpha animal has absolute leadership of the group. The leader of the pack has many privileges such as being the first to eat. It is not punished for biting (correcting) its subordinates if it considers their behavior inappropriate, and everyone stays out of its way. In principle, puppies see their master as their alpha dog because, by nature, a human being towers over a dog and is therefore the dominant one. It is not until the master transmits signals that confuse the dog, that it starts to doubt the sit-

Dogs are pack animals.

uation. He could then try, instinctively, to take over leadership of the family. This is noticeable when a dog becomes more disobedient and "bad-tempered." It might start to growl when its owner tries to groom it, for example or wants to sit where the dog is already sitting or lying. If the owner does not obey the dog, then the dog could try to correct the owner's behavior. Once it has reached that stage, the dog usually gets the blame – quite wrongly. The dog is merely following its instinct. In its eyes, the peace and safety of the pack is at risk due to this whimsical or indecisive leader figure, so it will want to take over the role.

Right:
Jack Russell
terrier.

You are the leader of the pack

As the owner of your new dog, you are its new alpha dog, its pack leader. All your dog requires of you is to be consistent and to set the limits. The knowledge that it is a member of a pack, however small, where the rules are clear, gives it a sense of security and peace. You are not only the leader of the pack during its upbringing, you will remain the leader of the pack for as long as your dog is part of your family.

Pack rules

- *Do not grant the dog free access to the whole house*
  This is a privilege reserved for the other members of the family, who are higher in rank than the dog. Certain rooms of the house, such as an entire upper floor, should be consistently taboo.

- *Do not feed the dog until everyone else has eaten*
  Those higher in rank always eat first. You could also feed your dog at completely different times to your own mealtimes.

- *Do not play with the dog when it tries to force you to do so*
  It is commanding you to pay attention to it, and in so doing is granting itself a higher ranking position. It is the pack leader who determines when the dog is to be stroked or played with, and for how long.

In your dog's eyes you are the leader of its pack.

- *Never walk toward the dog to stroke or cuddle him*
  ... always call it to come to you.

- *Never lie on the ground with the dog, always keep your face higher than the dog's head*
  Higher-ranking pack members will never adopt a position that is literally lower than a lower ranking pack member.

The master decides when the game is over.

- *Never let your dog "win" at games*
  Don't interfere with its toys but keep separate toys to play dog-and-master games, that are put away when the game is over – if you give them back to the dog, it will have "won."

- *Always walk ahead, the dog will follow you*
  You should not allow the dog to determine where the walk takes you, leave the house or enter another room first. The pack leader always leads the way, the lower ranking pack members must follow the leader.

Taking its food away?

Until recently, it was thought that a pack leader should be able to take a bone or food away from a dog. This is not so. In the wild, lower ranking wolves in a pack are always keep what they have managed to forage. You can teach your dog to let you take its food away, however. While the dog is still young, regularly remove its food bowl, add a special treat (such as a piece of liver sausage or cheese) and give the bowl back straight away. The dog will soon learn that its bowl being taken away only has its advantages and you will avoid it growling or snarling at mealtimes, without any confrontation – or worse!

Teach your children that the dog is not a toy.

Children and ranking

Although Jack Russells usually get along well with kids, much will depend on how the children treat the dog and the experience the dog has had with children. In principle, most dogs will not see children under the age of about nine as "higher ranking" and will tolerate about as much from them as they would from young puppies. But there are exceptions. Not all the problems that can occur with children are necessarily the result of a ranking problem. It goes without saying that you must teach your children that the new housemate is not a toy, that they mustn't tease it or pick it up and carry it everywhere, its legs have a purpose. Never leave a child and a dog alone together, however trustworthy the dog may be or may seem. In their innocence or curiosity, a child could inadvertently hurt a dog – you can imagine what the consequence might be. The opposite can also happen. A young Jack Russell is very playful and has extremely sharp little teeth. Screaming children running around all over the place are, of course, simply begging to be chased. Fun and laughter all round, but your dog will only get even more excited, thinking that the children are playing with it. A dog has no hands, so it "holds" the children with its sharp teeth. The result is crying children, a complaining owner, and a bewildered little dog who just doesn't understand what is going on. In practice, it is not possible to watch over dog and children all the time. To avoid mishaps, it is best to put the dog in the crate or in another room if play seems to be getting too boisterous.

To avoid disturbing the relationship between your children
and the dog, teach your children that they must:
- always call the dog to them and never walk (or worse still, crawl) to the dog;
- leave the dog alone when it is eating or sleeping;
- not give the dog any commands unless there is an adult present;
- not lie on the floor with the dog;
- never stare the dog straight in the eye;
- leave the dog's food bowl, chews, and toys alone;
- never play any confrontational games with the dog – so no games that your dog might consider as fights.

    Tracking games and retrieval are quite safe in this respect.

Many bite accidents and problems with dogs can be attributed to a mis-interpretation of the dog's body language and behavior. You can learn all about this at good training classes, but a wide range of good publications on the subject of body language is also available – use them to your advantage.

9 WHAT YOU NEED TO KNOW ABOUT SOCIALIZATION AND UPBRINGING

The socialization phase

An important phase in the life of any dog is the socialization phase, that occurs at around 7 and 14 weeks old. In this relatively short time, impressions will remain with it for the rest of its life. If the dog has an unfortunate experience with cats, for instance, there is a very good chance that it will have difficulty getting on with cats for the rest of its life.

The same rule applies to positive experiences. For the whole of its life the dog will react positively to anything with which it became familiar in this early phase. So not only should your puppy gain lots of new experiences, they should be as pleasant as possible.

An ounce of prevention....

If you live in the country, your dog will almost automatically get used to tractors and cattle, etc., but may seldom encounter buses, elevators, busy traffic, and suchlike, so it is important that you acquaint it with these too. Some people find it unimportant to socialize their dog with situations that are irrelevant to their circumstances at that particular point in time.

Socializing in
practice.

Because they don't like cats, owners may not bother to socialize the dog with cats, and if they don't have a driver's license or an automobile, they think their dog does not need to be familiar with riding in an automobile. Remember, however, that the socialization phase is an imprinting exercise that will remain with the dog for the rest of its life, for at least another twelve years in other words, and nobody can see into the future. And an ounce of prevention is worth a pound of cure.

Socializing in practice

Don't make fuss too much about new situations, as this could suggest something "scary" or "strange," just introduce them to the dog in a very matter-of-fact way, as something quite ordinary. Take you puppy out near a busy road, and don't stop if it reacts nervously. Just walk on, giving a slight jerk on the leash to encourage the puppy to do the same. In all other situations, you should ensure that you reflect your self-confidence in your puppy. Do not react any differently to the way you would without your dog. You are its role model so it will automatically

You are its shining example and role model.

adopt your matter-of-fact attitude. But beware of exposing your puppy to too many new experiences at once, as this could have an adverse effect and cause the dog to become nervous and unhappy with new situations.

Negative experiences during the socialization phase

In an ideal world, all your puppy's new experiences would be fun and positive, but the world is not ideal so there is a real chance of something negative happening during the socialization phase. Your puppy might get scratched by a cat, frightened by a scooter screeching over the sidewalk, or have some child tugging at its ears – such situations can't always be avoided. However, you can ensure that the occurrence makes less of an impression on your pup. Your attitude is crucial. In any unpleasant situation, you must react calmly, act as completely unaffected as possible. Do not pick the dog up, don't scream or shout, don't comfort it, in short, don't make an issue of it. Just imagine how your puppy must be feeling. If you, its role model, are clearly upset by the situation, then this has got to be extremely threatening. You sometimes hear people saying that a dog is scared of big black dogs, or a particular breed of dog, because it has had a traumatic experience with one in the past. It is usually not so much the event itself as the way in which the owner reacted to what happened that will largely determine the way in which the dog will respond in future.

Raising your dog

Consistency

The key to successfully raising your dog and your interaction with it is consistency. As you saw in the chapter on Rank, dogs are happier if the rules are clear. Before your puppy actually

Not allowed? Offer it a safe and more enjoyable alternative.

moves in, you ought to discuss the do's and don'ts with the family, i.e. what the puppy will be allowed to do and what it will not. Anything you permit must always be permitted, and anything you disallow must never be allowed. It sounds simple but the practice proves much harder than the theory. As an example, you all agree that the puppy is not to be given any food from the table because you detest scrounging dogs. But your children give it the occasional tidbit from the table and, because it's the dog's birthday, or you give it a piece of cake when you have coffee. So the rule has not been consistently observed and now your dog will habitually sit and wait hopefully for any treat in the offing. The fact that it only ever gets something very occasionally actually makes it even more persistent because it has learned that it's being dogged that works – and Jack Russell terriers are decidedly dogged! As another example, you allow your dog to sit on the sofa. One day, it comes in from a digging session in the garden just as you have "important" company who are sitting on the sofa. The dog comes bounding into the living room, leaps onto the sofa, cheerfully greeting your guests in passing, and leaves its muddy pawprints all over their clothes. You send it away in anger, but it naturally doesn't understand why. So think about the effect and feasibility of your rules before your actually enforce them. Your Jack Russell cannot be expected to appreciate mood changes and circumstances that cause you to allow something one day, and disallow it the next. Irritating behavior and disobedience are often blamed on a dog when it is almost always a result of inconsistency on the part of the owner and the owner's family. It is by no means easy to be consistent, but your efforts will be rewarded with interest by a happy, obedient dog who recognizes your limits – and therefore its own – and, in time, it will refrain from overstepping them.

The value of praise

Your dog will not automatically know what behavior you will or will not tolerate. You will have to make that clear by praising it when it does something right. This might sound simple enough, but in practice it is not, in fact, it is no easier than being consistent. It is important to praise the dog at the right time so that the puppy can make the link between your approval and the desired behavior. Suppose you command it to sit down and it does actually start to do just that. As it looks as if it is going to do what you have asked him to do, you praise it – but you praise it too soon. The dog now thinks you are satisfied with it merely bending its back legs a little. Praise is also often given too late and that makes it equally ineffective. Praise should be clearly recognized as such. You can praise your dog by saying "Good boy/girl" in a louder voice that you would usually use, by rewarding it with a pat on the head or stroking it, or giving it a piece of cheese or some other treat. A combination would, of course, get your message across even more clearly. Remember that Parson and Jack Russell terriers are extremely lively and too much enthusiastic praise is likely to make them over-excited. Try to find a happy medium.

Make sure your dog understands what you mean.

Punishment?

Punishment only has any effect at all in "caught-in-the-act" situations. Childishly simple, you might well say, but in practice it doesn't quite seem to work out that way. As an illustration of bad timing, let's take the leashed Jack Russell terrier that lets fly at a cat. Very few owners will anticipate this in time to be able to punish the dog before it actually attacks; the cat, therefore, will have long since escaped and the dog will have discovered just how much fun chasing cats can be. Because it enjoyed it so much, it'll try it again next time. If you punish it afterward, you won't really bother it, the fun was worth it. If you punish it before it has even had a chance to chase the cat, it will not have had time to have any fun, the exact opposite, in fact. It will not bother to let attack cats in future, since just thinking about it led to a harsh reprimand and it didn't even get the reward of seeing the cat run away. The degree and manner of punishment is something else to be considered. It is not uncommon to find an owner who thinks that he or she is punishing the dog by vaguely jerking at the

... that was fun! It was even worth the punishment!

leash, but the dog doesn't actually experience this as a punishment and simply continues the same, undesirable behavior: the owner is not being clear enough. Equally confusing is the owner who talks reassuringly when the dog is displaying undesirable behavior: "You don't have to bark like that, it's only a little pussycat, don't be silly," and even stroking the dog at the same time. This will not help the dog to understand that you find its behavior unacceptable. It is more likely to encourage the dog, in fact, because it sees the reassuring talking and stroking as a reward or encouragement. Habitual behavior problems are often the result of the owner's bad timing or vagueness. Punishment only has the desired deterrent effect if it is administered at the start of the undesirable behavior and is "harsh" enough.

"Guilty" behavior

Destructive behavior is relatively common in young puppies, when they are cutting their second teeth and have become "teenagers." Dogs often grow out of these bad habits. It is pointless punishing your dog for damaging something while you've been away; it will not link your punishment to the damage, but will be a little nervous and somewhat dejected when you come home in future – its body language and facial expression, with which it expresses fear, submissiveness, and confusion, is sadly often interpreted as "guilty" behavior. Rather than punishing the dog for something it has done wrong, you'd do better not to give it the opportunity. In a crate, it cannot do any damage so you can always say "good boy" when you come home. Give it tasty chews and toys as a

Learning and socializing should not be forced.

means of both killing time and satisfying its need to chew. In some cases, a dog will develop destructive behavior out of sheer boredom. Give it plenty of alternatives by taking different routes when out walking, or playing different ball and tracking games; that way, it will be less inclined to dream up its own entertainment. Right from the word go, make sure that there is something in it for the dog if it walks close to you when your are out, focusing its attention on you. You can do this by occasionally giving it a treat "for no apparent reason" or playing with it just for fun. This will prevent its attention straying to other things.

How to administer punishment

If your dog does something that really goes beyond your limits, shout "NO!" loudly, and in a strong, low, and angry tone of voice. You should be standing as close to the dog as possible. The idea is to really frighten it with your verbal correction. If this doesn't work, because it is too far away from you, throw something toward it that will make a lot of noise. Again, the idea is really scare it. The advantage of the latter is that it will not even associate the fright with your presence. Once your dog, still recovering from the shock, stops what it was doing call it cheerfully to come to you and offer it an alternative to its undesirable behavior, such as a ball game or a treat. It will soon think twice before displaying that behavior in future because of your terrible displeasure last time and the fright it got.

Picking a puppy up by the scruff of its neck and giving it a good shake is still often seen as a clear method of punishment, but dogs only ever do that to prey they want to kill. No dog will ever correct another dog that way! So don't ever do it either, it will do more than anything else to damage the trusting relationship between you.

What's on the other side?

10 BASIC TRAINING

Getting used to a collar and leash

Your puppy will probably never have worn a collar before it came to live with you, so its fierce protests, when you try and put a collar on for the first time, are hardly surprising. If you put it on just before you feed it or play with it, the distraction will make it easier for it to accept this restraint. Once your pup is used to wearing a collar, usually only a matter of days, you can attach a lightweight leash to it, but do not hold onto the

What on earth is this?

Now, let's see who's strongest.

leash as yet. Again, distract it with a game or a treat when you first put the leash on. Initially, just leave the leash dangling on the collar, but keep an eye on the dog's behavior. If its reaction to the lead trailing along behind it is not (or no longer) negative, you can put it on the leash and hold onto the other end. If it starts to protest, lure it toward you with sweet talk and/or treats. The process of acclimatizing the terrier to the collar and leash usually only takes a couple of days and if you encourage and distract it calmly but cheerfully, eventually it will not mind wearing them.

Important tips for successfully raising your Jack Russell or Parson

➤ **Be consistent**
Do not withdraw a command once you have given it and never accept a command that has only been half-obeyed. Always end the training session by rewarding an exercise well done.

➤ **Don't expect too much**
Your puppy is playful and easily distracted. You cannot (yet) ask it to "stay" sitting or lying still for five minutes. Only make it stay for a few seconds and extend this time gradually. For the first few months, the training sessions should only last five or ten minutes at a time. Make sure your dog enjoys the exercises to keep it motivated

➤ **Be clear**
Pronounce the command clearly, saying the dog's name first so that it knows you are talking to it.

➤ **Choose the right moment and the right place**
If your puppy is distracted when you give it a command, it is very likely that it will not register. Make sure you have its full attention before you command it to do something. Do not try to train your pup just after it has eaten, has a full bladder, or is very sleepy. Take your puppy somewhere quiet, with as few distractions as possible to perform the exercises.

➤ **You decide when an exercise has ended, not the puppy.**
If you tell it to sit and it cheerfully gets up again after a couple of seconds, then it will have ended the exercise itself. But it is not up to your dog to do that, you must end the exercise yourself by saying "free" or "okay" or something similar, and saying it at the right moment.

↞ Do not repeat yourself

If a puppy that is being told to sit hears: "Jacky sit, sit down, Jacky sit down, no, I said, sit, I mean it Jacky, sit," it will learn that it can ignore as many commands as it likes without being reprimanded. Unfortunately, other commands such as "come" are often communicated this way. A command given repeatedly in a short space of time loses its meaning. Attract your puppy's attention and give the command just once, loudly and clearly, when you are sure you have your puppy's undivided attention.

Come

You can practice the command "come" either indoors or outside in the garden. Wait until your puppy looks at you, then crouch down and cheerfully, invitingly and clearly say: "Come." Your puppy will be even more interested in coming to you if you pat the ground in front of you with the flat of your hand when you call it. If your puppy comes toward you, encourage it. Once it has reached you, it is a "Good Boy!" of course. Teaching your dog to come to you is extremely simple if you bear in mind that coming to you should always be fun. So don't call it to you then punish it, and don't only call it when it's time to put it back on the leash to go home or into the crate. You should avoid your puppy thinking of you as a spoilsport as this will ensure it no longer wants to come to you when you call. While you are out walking, make a habit of calling your dog to you every so often and giving it a biscuit, or playing with it before walking it home.

There is no point in giving it a command if it is obviously not paying attention.

Sit

Hold a treat above your puppy's nose, move it slowly toward the back of its head, saying "Sit" at the same time. In principle, it will have to sit if it is to be able to reach the biscuit and that is what most dogs do – once the owner gets the knack of it, at least. If it does sit then, of course, it will get both the biscuit and your praise. Once it has realized what is required of it on hearing the command "sit," you can leave the biscuit out.

Lying down on command

Teach your dog this command from the sitting position. Hold a treat in your closed fist in front of its nose so that it can smell it. Now lower your fist, saying "Down" at the same time. Interested in that nice smell, your puppy will follow the movement of your fist. The closer to the ground your puppy gets, the more your hand should start to open. As soon as the dog is actually lying down, open your hand completely so that it can get at the treat, and praise it.

"Sit" is an easily taught basic exercise.

It is a good idea to teach your puppy to sit at every curb. This will teach it that a curb is a sort of boundary at which it cannot automatically go "forward." This will take an awful lot of time and patience to start with but with a view to its safety and that of other road-users and pedestrians, it is certainly a lesson worth learning.

Teaching the dog to sit at every curb is very time-consuming but could save its life.

In principle you can teach your dog almost anything using this "treat-in-a-fist-method," from rolling over to walking on its hind legs. It is important, however, that you always observe the same basic principles. Be very clear and only reward it once it has actually done what you commanded it to do – no sooner and no later.

Tasty treats will do the trick.

11 GENERAL CARE

Caring for a smooth coat

Caring for the coat of a smooth-haired Jack Russell terrier is not usually difficult. The dirt-repellent coat lies close to the skin. When the dog is molting, the loose hairs are most effectively removed with a rubber brush or massage glove. Most Jack Russells have longer hairs in the tip of the tail and in the groin. These can be cut to keep the dog looking "groomed."

Rubber massage glove

Left:
Slicker brush for rough coats

Right:
Stripping knife

Caring for a rough coat

Just like the smooth coat, it is also fairly easy to care for a rough coat. Preferably use a small slicker brush with short pins. When brushing your dog, be careful not to damage the coat and avoid any areas of thin hair so as not to harm your dog's skin with the uncoated metal pins.

Brushing the dog once a week will normally be adequate. Depending on the quality of the coat, a rough-haired dog will need to be stripped two or three times a year. Stripping means pulling out the old hairs by hand to allow the new hairs to grow. It is easy to tell whether or not a coat is ready for stripping by pinching a clump of hairs on the shoulders and pulling it in the direction of growth. If the hair comes out easily then the coat is ready for stripping. If not, wait a while longer. Some Jack Russells have a softer, woolly coat that is difficult to strip. Do not be tempted to allow that kind of coat structure to be shaven, however as this will not remove the old hairs from the coat. The old hairs will simply stay in the shaft and make it difficult for new hairs to grow through. This will just make it even harder to care for the coat properly. A softer coat structure often improves once the coat has been professionally stripped once or twice.

Some rough-haired Jack Russells have longer hairs in between the pads of their paws. That can be awkward, because dirt, tiny stones, and ice can get caught in the hair. Cut away this hair regularly, preferably with a pair of curved nail-scissors, holding the curve toward the paw so that you don't hurt your dog.

Washing

Despite having a predominantly white coat, Jack Russell terriers do not get dirty very easily. If the dog does get dirty leave it to dry first, making sure that it is not in a draft. Once it has dried it is quite easy to brush the excess dirt out of its coat using a hard, bristle brush. If your dog has really gone to town, it might need a bath. For this, always use a special dog shampoo. A good dog shampoo will not harm the sebum that protects the skin and the hair. Other shampoos, even baby shampoos, will leave the coat and skin more vulnerable and the coat will get dirty more quickly. Before you start washing it, you can put a large piece of cotton wool in each of its ears to stop the water getting in. Lather the shampoo in thoroughly and rinse it out again even more thoroughly. Use one or more fluffy towels to rub it as dry as possible and leave it to dry off somewhere nice and warm and away from a draft.

Pedicure

Long nails are not only unattractive, they can also be a hindrance to the dog walking. It could even develop an abnormal gait and its toes, which are usually close together, could start to separate. What is more, long nails break more easily and that is very painful.

Remember that the flesh continues to grow under the nails. The longer a dog walks around with nails that are too long, the longer the "quick" will be and the harder it will be to cut the nails painlessly and without any bleeding. Starting from an

Plucking out the hairs

Left: The coat is ready for stripping if the hair on top comes out easily

Right: The old hair can be pulled out by hand – pinched between your thumb and finger ...

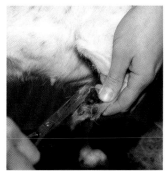

Left: ... or with a blunt stripping knife

Right: Cut away the excess hair sticking out between the pads of its paws

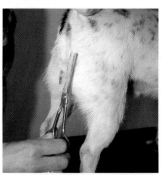

Left: The long hair on its "pants" can be cut shorter ...

Right: ... as can the long hair at the back of its tail

As a "finishing touch" the long hair at the tip of the tail is twisted and cut off

early age, it is therefore best to make a habit of keeping your dog's nails short. Preferably use a good pair of canine nail clippers. If the very thought of clipping your dog's nails sends shivers down your spine, have it done at a professional grooming parlor, or ask your vet as the occasion arises.

Teeth

All puppies have milk teeth. Between 4 and 6 months, the milk teeth make way for the permanent, adult teeth. The phase during which the puppies cut their second teeth is notorious. Some puppies will lose their appetite and most will have an increased need to chew and be inclined to chew things to bits. So make sure your puppy has plenty of safe things to chew on. This will help prevent it from satisfying its chewing needs on your furniture or shoes. Occasionally, one or more milk teeth do not fall out, making it difficult for the underlying second tooth to come through normally. Some teeth can grow crooked as a result. So it makes sense to keep an eye on the process so that you can take any necessary action in good time. This doesn't only apply to puppies, either. It is also a good idea to inspect an adult dog's teeth regularly.

Initially, tatar will form on the rear molars in particular. This can lead to decay, infections, and even loss of teeth. In addition, rotten teeth will cause bad breath. You can clean a light scaling easily enough yourself with a baby's toothbrush or a

Cutting the dog's nails is no luxury; it's a necessity.

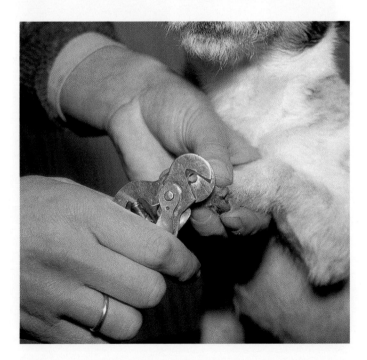

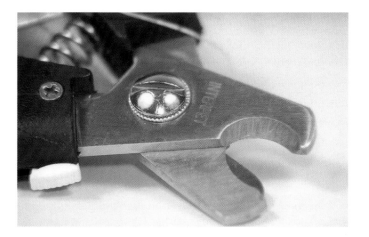

Good nail clippers make an excellent investment.

piece of special canine gauze with a little child's toothpaste spread on it. A heavy coating of tatar can be removed at the grooming parlor where they use a special scraper. If your dog is not exactly easy-going in this respect, or if the tartar has been allowed to build up too much, the only option left is for the vet to remove it under general anesthetic. So try to stop it getting that far by checking your dog's teeth regularly. Chewing on tough bones and suchlike will prevent tartar from building up in most cases, but sometimes this will not be enough, because certain family lines are more prone to producing tartar than others.

Auditory canal

The auditory canal in a Jack Russell is seldom the source of any problems. The consequences of developing an ear infection are nonetheless serious, so it makes sense to inspect the auditory canal at least once a week.

Remove any excess of earwax and, of course, sand or dirt, using a special canine ear-cleaner, gently cleaning the dirt released with a soft tissue. A dog's auditory canal is not straight as it is

Left:
Healthy, adult teeth

Right:
Teeth with a little scale on them

in humans, it has a bend in it. You are therefore strongly advised against using cotton buds, which usually only push the dirt down further into the canal, enabling a deeper, insidious infection to develop. If your dog has a granular, dark, and smelly discharge from its ears, then it probably has ear-mites. Most dogs suffering from ear-mites scratch their ears a lot. It is fairly simple to cure and there are various effective products on the market, available from any vet.

Fleas

There is not a dog alive that manages to stay completely flea-free for its entire life. Fleas are one of the most persistent parasites, and can survive in the egg or pupal stage for an extremely long time, sometimes for years. You may be sure that for every flea on your dog, there are another 99 at some stage of development, be it egg, larva, or pupa, in your dog's environment, in its bed, crate, in the sofa, in the car, in every nook and cranny. Looking at the problem from that perspective, there is obviously little point in treating just the dog for fleas. If the pesticide is to have any effect at all, it must be used elsewhere as well. The best way to treat dogs with fleas is to use an effective flea spray or wash the dog with a good anti-flea shampoo. Don't forget to treat any other pets you might have as well. Everywhere the dog goes, which could therefore be infested with flea eggs, larvae, or pupae, should also be treated with a household flea spray. In addition, vacuuming regularly, preferably every day, will remove the food the flea larvae would feed on, thus drastically reducing their chances of survival. There is little point in washing the floor, as fleas actually prefer a moist environment and are immune to cleaning agents. Beside the conventional flea repellents, you can also give your dog tablets that sterilize any flea sucking your dog's blood thus making it impossible for the flea to reproduce. If you use them consistently they are effective but, in view of re-infection, you will still have to use the conventional anti-flea products from time to time. Your dog could still contract fleas from other dogs or cats, or bring them in from outside. Because puppies are particularly vulnerable, you must use an anti-flea product especially developed for puppies, which you can buy from a pet store or your vet.

Worming treatment

Various types of worm are common in dogs. The best-known are roundworms, tapeworms, and hookworms. All puppies, whether the mother has been wormed or not, have round-worms. A responsible breeder will already have treated the pups for worms several times before they go to their new owners. You will usually receive a worming schedule from the breeder, stating which worming product should be used and when. If you stick to this schedule you shouldn't have a problem.

Tapeworms use fleas as an intermediary host. If your dog has fleas, there is a good chance it also has a tapeworm infection. You can recognize them by the tapeworm segments that look like grains of rice in the feces or around the anus. A neglected worm infection is not entirely harmless for the dog concerned, and even a lightly infected dog could infect young children, with worrying health problems as a result. To treat or prevent worm infections, it is important that you worm your adult dog at least once every six months. For adult dogs, an effective worming product twice a year will usually suffice. This should preferably be a broad-spectrum worming preparation that will kill all the types of worm found in dogs.

Ticks

Ticks are anything but innocent parasites, they live off the blood of animals and humans alike. They lie in wait in tall grass and undergrowth, waiting for a warm-blooded passer-by to get their hooks into. Once they have attached themselves to their victim and sucked themselves full of blood, the parasites are easy to recognize as round, gleaming gray warts on the skin. It is estimated that some 15 to 25% of the ticks are infected with the bacteria that causes Lyme disease, and this can create chronic health problems for the tick's host – and that goes for humans too. To prevent your dog from being bitten, you are advised to use a tick collar or spray. Should you nevertheless find a tick on your dog, remove it as quickly as possible. If it is removed within 24 hours, the risk of infection is practically negligible. Remove the tick by grasping it as close to the skin of the dog as possible, holding a pair of tweezers or between your thumb and finger, and pull it straight out in one go. Make sure that no part of the tick is left in the skin and disinfect the wound with a little iodine. Dog owners used to be advised to first numb the tick with alcohol but it has since been discovered that this actually increases the risk of infection.

12 FOOD

Commercially prepared food

As it is practically impossible to prepare a balanced food from scratch, the best thing to do is to give your dog commercially prepared food. The food should not only contain all the right nutrients, minerals, and vitamins, they also have to be in the right proportions. The better brands of dog food guarantee both a complete and a well-balanced diet. Your dog will get everything it needs, but not too much of anything, if you give it a complete dog food and nothing but that. If you give it biscuits or a dinner, you can also let it have a meat day once a week, giving it a complete meat meal (frozen canine dinner) or meat only such as variety meats (liver, lungs, heart). Its intestinal flora can benefit from a meat day. Another alternative is to only give it complete, frozen dog food. This diet actually resembles its natural diet most closely and is,

Left:
Dry biscuits

Right:
Complete dog food

without a doubt, very healthy. Make sure that the meal really is "complete" and not meat only, as that will certainly give rise to health problems in time.

Which brand or type of food?
When buying food, make sure that it is a complete food, because there are some foods on the market that still need other ingredients to be added, such as a dinner without any meat in it and certain types of canned foods.
It is an indication of quality for the manufacturer and, of course, to the food itself if only natural preservatives have been used. But don't be fooled by such formulas as: "No chemical preservatives or colorings added." A manufacturer is some-

Right:
Jack Russell terrier

times allowed to print this on the package even if the ingredients used in the food contain such chemicals. The statement is quite true in that these preservative and colorings weren't added in the factory – because they were already in the basic ingredients when they arrived there! Most breeders know their way around in the dog-food world. They will usually have had years of experience and will be quite capable of advising you on which sort and brand of food would best suit your terrier. As a rule, your breeder will advise you to choose a food with a relatively low protein content, to prevent your already energetic little dog becoming hyperactive. You can switch from puppy food, which usually has a relatively high protein content, to adult food, fairly soon too for the same reason. You can switch foods as early as four months. Dogs older than 7-8 years should be fed a food specifically developed for elderly dogs.

Additives

Adding extra calcium, oil, or other nutrients to dog food is a throwback to the time when the quality of commercially prepared dog foods was somewhat dubious. Nowadays, dog food is "big business" and the better brands perform extensive

A healthy dog in prime condition.

A food cube is a good idea for dogs that are over-weight:
they have to work to get their supper!

research to further improve the food that is already excellent as it is. In principle, you can safely assume there is no longer any such thing as a poor quality dog food. But neither is there a single brand or type of dog food that will suit all dogs. Food that helps dog A keep its glossy coat and reach old age without any health problems worth speaking of, could cause all kinds of allergic reactions and other problems for dog B. If your dog is not doing well on a particular type or brand of food, don't resort immediately to a food supplement. Dog food is perfectly balanced and contains all the nutrients your dog requires, in the right proportions. Adding your own supplements will only upset this delicate balance with what could be detrimental consequences. Calcium supplements are particularly notorious in this respect as too much calcium will lead to calcification of the joints. Too high a protein content is equally disastrous, as this will put too much of a strain on the kidneys, which could lead to premature kidney failure. It can also cause increased (or hyper) activity. Too high a protein content is often the result of mixing meat or canned food with a complete dry dog food or dinner. It's only natural for a dog to enjoy that kind of mix more than its dry biscuits, but while people like cakes and cookies too, everyone knows they should not be considered as good nutrition. If your dog appreciates the flavor of its food, that's a bonus, but remember that it absolutely no guarantee that the food is genuinely nutritious.

Condition

If your dog's condition leaves a little (or a lot) to be desired, if it is producing too many feces or they are too soft, if it is molting a lot or there are any other signs that might indicate an adverse reaction to its food, first consult a vet. Several simple tests could exclude any medical grounds for the symptoms. If your dog is otherwise healthy, then gradually switch to a different type or brand of food. For example, dogs with skin problems often benefit from a diet in which lamb is the only source of protein, but the root of the problem can sometimes be the preservative used, and switching to a food that contains no chemical preservatives will then do the trick.

> **Tip**
> Never give your dog fresh pork products as they could be infected with Aujeszky's disease, which is fatal to dogs.

Portions

Because pups only have tiny stomachs, their daily requirement should be divided into four or five portions. Gradually increase the portions and reduce the meals to two a day. Adult dogs are also best fed twice a day. Two smaller portions will be digested better than one large one. And as mealtimes are one of the highlights of almost every dog's day, why not give it that pleasure twice?
There is no unequivocal ruling as regards the amount you should feed your dog. The daily requirement varies depending

on the type of food and on the dog itself. Even dogs of the same weight and sex, getting the same amount of exercise, will not necessarily have the same daily feeding requirement. So your dog's feeding requirement could well differ from the recommended daily amount stated on the pack.

Too fat?

Jack Russell terriers do not have a great tendency to grow fat – luckily. Excess body weight is a strain on the system and the organs, such as the heart, and shortens the life expectancy. So keep a good eye on your dog's "waistline." A general guideline: if you can easily feel your dog's ribs through its coat, then your dog is not too fat. If you really have to "push" to feel its ribs, on the other hand, it is overweight. If in doubt, consult a vet.

A dog that is too fat will benefit from more exercise and a (slight) change of diet, so no more snacks and smaller portions perhaps. If your dog is still hungry then you can give it as many green beans as it likes. Green beans will satisfy it without putting an ounce of flesh on.

Do not allow your dog to get too fat.

Average weight of an adult dog:	
Parson Jack Russell terrier	13 – 14 lbs
Jack Russell terrier	11 – 12 lbs

Right:
Most Jack
Russells have a
good appetite.

Spoiled or sick?

Sometimes a dog will refuse the food its owner puts down for it. This is usually because the owner has been too indulgent and the Jack Russell realises that it can expect to receive something else (i.e. something tastier but less healthy) if it shows little interest in what is in its bowl. If this happens, do not indulge your dog by giving it an alternative meal. A day of fasting will certainly not do it any harm, and its appetite will usually return the next day.

But there could be a medical reason why the dog is refusing food. While they are cutting their second teeth between the ages of four and six months, for example, a lot of dogs will lose their appetite. It is quite possible that your dog's teeth are bothering it. More serious reasons are that it has a foreign body in its stomach, a temperature, or some other reason for not feeling well, and is therefore eating very little, if at all. If you are at all worried about why your dog is off its food, consult the vet.

Dangerous snacks

Do not give your dog chicken or other poultry bones, or the bones of pork or game birds. They splinter and can damage its digestive system. Marrow bones are not as innocent as they look, either. Although they do not splinter, they can get stuck round your Jack Russell's lower jaw.

Marrowbones are
tasty treats but
their shape
makes them a
potential danger.

13 EXERCISE AND ACTIVITY

Hunting

Despite being specifically bred for fox-hunting, Jack Russell terriers are not actually used for hunting very often anymore. Not many people are engaged in hunting these days anyway and hunting is now so tightly controlled by strict regulations and licenses that some people who might otherwise be interested are discouraged before they even start. If the idea of hunting with your dog appeals to you, contact a hunting club in your area and they will be only too happy to give you more information.

Sporting activities

Jack Russell terriers are active, sporting little dogs, and therefore ideal candidates for certain canine sports. The most suitable sports are fly-ball and agility tests, although you won't find many Parsons or Jacks at the top of the latter field. Their class is dominated by Shelties and other shepherd dogs that have a stronger will to please. It is, nevertheless, great fun to compete and can be just as exciting for both dog and master, even if you don't reach the national finals. Practically all dogs

Jack Russell racing is fun for dog and master alike.

of both breeds are also excellent trackers and even a first obedience course is an option – Jack Russells and Parsons are extremely intelligent and if their exercises are enjoyable enough, they can go a long way. These dogs are less suitable for the more advanced obedience classes, however, as they demand a far greater will to please than you could expect from practically any terrier.

Retrieval

It is fairly easy to teach your Jack to retrieve various objects. If it is walking around with something in its mouth, crouch down and enthusiastically call: "Fetch!" If it comes up to you with its toy, take it with one hand while offering it a treat with the other. In effect you will be "trading." If it gives you the toy and takes the treat, praise it. Throw the toy away again and say: "Fetch!" It will soon get the idea. If you catch your dog walking around with something in its mouth that it is not allowed to have, don't punish it, but say "fetch" in the same cheerful manner and exchange whatever it's holding in its mouth for a biscuit. Then throw something that it is allowed to have. That way, retrieval will still be a fun game to play without any negative associations.

Retrieving and swimming: Two perfect kinds of exercise.

Hide-and-seek

Rather than taking your dog to official tracking classes you can just play hide-and-seek with it in and around the home. The advantage of this is that you can play indoors and lay down your own rules. Tracking is an intensive activity for any dog and a Parson or Jack Russell terrier will definitely see it as a challenge. Indoors, you can hide its favorite ball under a pillow, for example. Don't make the game too hard to start with, give it a chance to figure out how to play.

Show it the ball, "hide" it under a pillow, and then tell it "Go find." If it gets the ball, reward it, and exchange the ball for a piece of cheese or some other treat. You can gradually increase the degree of difficulty, eventually hiding the ball while your dog isn't looking.

Another tracking game to play, either indoors or out, is "cloth sorting." You need four identical pieces of cloth. Two of which you carry around for a while in your pants pocket so that they can take on your scent. Lay one of these "scented cloths" on the ground and the two unscented cloths about 18 inches away from it. Now take the other cloth out of your pants pocket and let your dog have a good sniff at it. Tell it to "Go find" which one of the three cloths has that same specific scent. It should retrieve the right cloth and if it does, you obviously praise it abundantly. You could bury its favorite ball in the garden or yard or on the beach and tell it to find it.

So you see, there are dozens of variations of hide-and-seek that you could devise, all of which would be equally enjoyable for both you and your terrier, and none of which would take much time or preparation.

Where's the ball gone?

Ah! There it is!

Now, I'll just dig some more ...

... gotcha!

Occupational therapy

There will be days when your Jack Russell is simply bubbling over with energy but you don't have enough time to keep it busy. Special toys have been developed that do just that. They tempt it to play, keeping it interested and occupied without taking up any of your time. One of the best games is a ball or cube with an opening into which you can push a few dog biscuits. Every so often, as the ball or cube rolls over, a biscuit will fall out. These kinds of game are great fun for any dog and particularly for Parson and Jack Russell terriers. Marketed under various brand names, they are available in a whole range of colors and sizes.

A food cube or ball works wonders when the master has no time to play.

Tip
Digging has just got to be the number one hobby of any right-minded Jack Russell terrier. If you have a beautifully laid out garden, this could prove to be a major source of irritation. Breaking this bad habit is hard, if not impossible. A far better solution is to create a sandpit especially for your Jack Russell and to teach it that it is allowed to dig there. If you initially hide a few biscuits or a toy in the sand, it will soon get the idea.

Swimming

Jack Russells are hardy little dogs that won't let the odd downpour prevent them from playing outside. Your average terrier will thoroughly enjoy swimming or paddling in shallow water and it is good exercise as well. No extra measures need be taken on warm days, but if you let your dog swim on a cold day, always take a towel with you and dry it off well. Never leave your dog to dry in a draft as that will make any dog ill, even a breed as hardy as the Jack Russell terrier. Before you let your dog swim, check that the water is safe enough for it to do so. Banks that are too steep for it to climb in and out easily, long

Water is a fun way of cooling down on hot days.

stringy water plants, fishing nets, and undercurrents are all potentially dangerous.

Safety in the car

Whenever you take your dog anywhere in the car, the preferred means of transport is a crate. Keeping the dog in a dog safety-belt in the back seat is an excellent alternative. It is not safe to have a dog loose in the car or in the back of a pickup truck. Not only could it make driving extremely difficult and therefore dangerous, in the event of an accident it would just be flung out of the car or truck.

A safe way to transport your dog.

14 ABNORMALITIES AND DISEASES

A healthy breed

Parson and Jack Russell terriers are generally healthy dogs with hardly any known breed-related genetic abnormalities. But of course there is always a possibility of your puppy or dog catching some kind of disease. There are various symptoms to look out for, such as continual vomiting, a high temperature, abnormal feces, little or no appetite, drinking more, drowsiness, or a different way of urinating. If you sense that there is something wrong with your dog, always consult a vet. It is a good idea to take its temperature beforehand, always rectally and preferably with a digital thermometer. The normal temperature of a dog at rest, is higher than in humans, somewhere between 99.5°F and 101.3°F.

Standard inoculations

Inoculations have been developed for a number of life-threatening canine diseases. These are distemper, parvo, hepatitis, leptospirosis, bordetella or kennel cough, corona, Aujeszky's disease, and rabies. With the exception of bordetella, corona, Aujeszky's disease, which are optional, it is usually standard for puppies to be vaccinated against all of these diseases. In the United States, rabies inoculations are compulsory. It is not yet possible to give young puppies all the necessary inoculations in one go, so it will have to have two or three shots, the last usually being given at around twelve weeks. So until then, a puppy will not be fully protected against these diseases and you are advised not to let your dog out in places where it runs the risk of becoming infected, such as a popular dog-walking route or dog toilet area. It is normal for a dog to have a booster shot every year to guarantee its continued protection. Every self-respecting breeder will give you an inoculation book, stating when and against what you puppy has been inoculated and when the shots should be repeated. If you observe the inoculation schedule strictly, then the risk of your dog suffering from any of these diseases will be practically negligible.

Kennel cough, rabies and Aujeszky's Disease
If you often go to places where there are a lot of dogs, such as contests or shows, it is well worth having your dog vaccinated or giving it nose drops against kennel cough. Kennel cough is an extremely contagious complaint, the typical symptom being long bouts of dry coughing. It can make puppies and older dogs particularly ill, as it is often accompanied by pneumonia or some other infection. In addition to the usual inoculations, most boarding kennels require dogs to have been inoculated by means of a shot or nose drops against kennel

Where has my master gone?

cough. However, as yet there are no inoculations that will protect your dog against every known form of kennel cough. So although the chance is drastically reduced, there is still a possibility of an inoculated dog catching the disease.

Inoculation against rabies is obligatory in all hot countries in which rabies is endemic in the wild mammal population, and this includes the United States. Rabies shots must be given every six months to a year. Your vet will give you a form which you should have with you and be able to show on request if you travel out-of-state or abroad with your dog.

Your dog can contract Aujeszky's disease, which is fatal, by coming into contact with (the feces of) pigs or raw pork. If your dog is in a high-risk group, then you would certainly not be wasting your time or money having it inoculated, although even this inoculation cannot offer 100% protection.

Patella luxation

A knee disorder known as patella luxation (PL) is occasionally seen in (Parson) Jack Russell terriers. There are different types of PL in varying degrees. A mild form of PL will hardly bother a dog at all, but a dog whose kneecaps become dislocated when it walks or jumps around, and do not slip back into place or only do so with difficulty, will clearly be handicapped by its affliction.

The condition will often worsen as the dog grows older and it will become increasingly painful because the bone surfaces will continuously rub against each other. The dog could also suffer from water-on-the-knee (housemaid's knee). In serious cases of PL, an operation often provides some improvement. Because the condition can be genetic, any self-respecting breeder of (Parson) Jack Russell terriers will have its breeding dogs tested for PL. A veterinarian with experience of PL will quickly be able to diagnose the condition, based on a manual examination.

Anal sacculitis

Anal sacculitis, commonly known as blocked anal glands, is a common complaint. The anal glands are located on either side of the anus, approximately half an inch below the surface. Dogs suffering from blocked anal glands often itch a lot and will try to relieve the itching by dragging their bottom over the ground ("scooting"). A vet can manually express anal glands but this is also often done in a grooming parlor. It should be performed very skillfully though, incorrectly expressing the anal glands will only worsen the condition. Some dogs are more susceptible to anal sacculitis than others. In chronic cases, a solution may be to surgically remove the anal glands.

Pyometra

Pyometra, an infection of the uterus, is a common affliction, not breed-related, that can affect bitches aged four years and older. If pyometra is not treated in time, it can be fatal. There are two forms of pyometra, open and closed. In the open type there is a discharge from the vagina that makes it easy to spot

Who will play with us?

the condition in time. With the closed type, on the other hand, the discharge cannot drain outside the body so it accumulates inside the uterus. It is this latter type that is most dangerous. The symptoms are the same for both types. The bitch has a temperature, is drowsier than normal, and will drink more than usual. A course of antibiotics can sometimes cure the infection but if it recurs, it makes more sense to allow the vet to perform a hysterectomy.

Infection of the foreskin

Infection of the foreskin is a common complaint amongst dogs. It can be recognized by the greenish-yellow discharge from the foreskin. Contrary to uterine infections, an infection of the foreskin is not life-threatening. Usually, the dog will not be particularly bothered by it, but the nasty stains the discharge leaves on your furniture and carpets are not a pretty sight. The vet can give you a special ointment for daily treatment of the foreskin, possibly backed up by a course of tablets. In most cases though, the infection will recur, and castration will almost always be the only solution.

Travel sickness
Most dogs that suffer from travel sickness associate riding in the car with something negative, such as a visit to the vet, the grooming parlor, or boarding kennel. They then get so upset that they become nauseous and start vomiting. It will often help if you take a travelsick dog out for short trips only and with something enjoyable at the end of the ride, such a short drive to the park, the woods, or the beach. Prevention is always better than cure, however, so take a puppy out in the automobile regularly for short journeys and make sure there is some fun waiting for it when it gets to wherever it's going. Unfortunately, a few dogs will continue to get travel sick and medication may prove necessary, although luckily enough many of them will grow out of it around their first birthday.

Poisoning
You can only hope that it will never happen to your dog, but if it does ever happen it is vital that you recognize the symptoms of poisoning. These can vary, depending on what it is your dog has eaten. A poisoned dog can vomit, drool excessively, shake from head to toe, have bad diarrhea, possibly with severe abdominal cramps, become apathetic, or even lapse into a coma. Occasionally, you could find reddish marks on the skin, as in the case of it having rolled in poisoned ivy or poisoned oak. If there is any suspicion of poisoning, it is essential that you get your dog to the vet as quickly as possible.

 If you know what your dog has eaten (or drunk), take the package with you to the veterinary practice, if at all possible. The treatment will depend upon the type of poison and the wrong treatment could have an adverse effect. The word "poison" will often evoke thoughts of some deliberately hostile act but whilst this is too often the case, sadly enough, there are also other ways your dog could get poisoned. Eating the manure of recently wormed horses, for example, can be extremely poisonous, and many plants are also very poisonous to dogs.

Food allergies

It seems that an increasing number of dogs suffer from food allergies. The biggest problem is often finding out exactly which ingredient it is to which the dog has an allergic reaction. Often it turns out to be the type of protein, but it could just as easily be the preservative, coloring matter, or some other ingredient that is to blame. Symptoms can include red bumps on the belly, in the groins, and armpits, or the feces could be normal one moment and soft the next. A dog with a food allergy will itch, very often over its whole body, making the dog scratch a lot. If you suspect a food allergy, it is important to discover what it was that caused the allergic reaction. You could try giving it a different kind of food, one without chemical preservatives or colorings, or one in which lamb is the only source of animal protein, such as a lamb and rice diet. Lamb seldom causes an allergic reaction.

Special foods have also been developed for dogs with allergies, and most sufferers seem to benefit from eating them. Note that a dog with a food allergy should never be given anything to eat other than its specially adjusted diet because even a minimal amount of the ingredient to which it is allergic could spark off a severe reaction.

The manure of recently wormed horses can be poisonous to small dogs like the Jack Russell; never let it near such a substance.

Cherry laurel *(Prunus laurocerasus)*
Common foxglove *(Digitalis purpurea)*
Cyclamen
Daffodil *(Narcissus)*
Deadly nightshade *(Atropa belladonna)*
Dumb cane *(Dieffenbachia)*
Golden chain *(Laburnum)*
Holly *(Ilex aquifolium)*
Ivy *(Hedera)*
Meadow saffron *(Colchicum autumnale)*

Mistletoe *(Viscum)*
Mock orange *(Philadelphus)*
Mistletoe *(Viscum)*
Nightshade *(Solanum)*
Oleander *(Nerium ornithogalum)*
Poinsettia *(Euphorbia)*
Poison ivy
Poison oak
Sumac
Thorn apple *(Datura stramonium}*
Tulip *(Tulipa)*

Atopy

Another allergy common in dogs is atopy. Atopy is an allergic reaction to substances the dog breathes in. This could be anything from pollen to house mites and skin flakes. A vet can perform an allergy test to determine which substance(s) cause an allergic reaction in your dog, but the problem with atopy is that it is often extremely difficult to prevent the dog from breathing in the substance responsible. That certainly applies to skin flakes, human or animal, although frequent vacuuming, a suitably adjusted diet, and regular washing with a special shampoo, can at least offer some relief.

If a dog is suffering from atopy it will itch everywhere and consequently scratch a lot, particularly the head and ears, the legs, armpits, and groin. The disease will usually become evident between six months and three years of age.

*Jack Russell –
male puppy*

Other causes of itching

If your dog is obviously itching , the cause need not necessarily be an allergy. It could well be that it has mites. Mites cannot be seen with the naked eye but your vet will have a special light to enable him to determine whether or not these parasites are plaguing your dog. Fleas are another major source of itching. You won't always be able to find the fleas themselves on the dog because they manage to take cover in no time, but you will be able to see the telltale feces of the flea, tiny brownish black granules, in the coat. Some dogs can actually have severe reactions to mites or even a single fleabite. This means it is allergic to the parasites. Some dogs display symptoms that at first suggest an allergy, but turn out not to be allergenic at all. Their scratching can simply be caused by a lack of attention. If a dog scratches, it gets its owner's attention so it does so more and more frequently, in the hope that it will get more and more attention.

Some Parsons and Jack Russell terriers have been known to have a wool allergy. Woollen blankets in the basket and/or a woolen carpet could thus be the cause of allergic reactions.

15 BREEDING

Your family situation

As the owner of a bitch, you might have considered breeding her, maybe because friends and acquaintances would so love to have one of your dog's puppies, or perhaps you would just love to have one of her puppies yourself. If everything goes according to plan, a litter of puppies is an enjoyable and memorable experience, but it is also a huge responsibility, and sometimes a nuisance and it always involves extra work, lots of extra work. Puppies aren't just fun, they are noisy, and between them they can disrupt a place in seconds, moving your furniture around to suit their taste, and producing a never-ending flow of feces and urine for you to clean up day after day. The adorable vandals your bitch has brought into the world will control the house and your whole lifestyle for the next seven or eight weeks. Moreover, the puppies' first impressions, vitally important for the rest of their lives, will be of you and the way you treat them. You owe it to the puppies and to society in general to give them the best possible foundation. This demands a minimal basic knowledge of a puppy's mental development and canine behavior in general. Raising a litter of puppies is not what everybody is cut out to do. It takes a lot of time and effort but more importantly, it requires knowledge and dedication.

For the money?

Jack Russell terriers are popular little dogs and it is often not hard to find potential new owners for the puppies. This can sometimes tempt people to breed purely for the purpose of lining their pockets – and there just couldn't be a worse reason. The whole undertaking can actually involve considerable expense. The stud fee alone, and then there are the possible travel costs, pedigree applications, inoculations, and worming treatments, (supplementary) puppy feed, and the changes that have to be made to the home. All this can put quite a strain on the family budget. Jack Russell bitches don't usually have any problem in whelping but you can bet your bottom dollar it'll be your bitch that needs the expensive veterinary assistance, or your pups that can't make it without medication or medical intervention. Very occasionally, such a litter can end up a complete and utter drama. There is even the possibility that your bitch may encounter such severe problems during pregnancy or whelping that she herself can no longer be saved. This is, indeed, a very negative scenario, but it can happen and very few prospective breeders are aware of it. Whatever happens, few people have ever struck it rich breeding dogs.

In actual fact, as a breeder you will need some savings put by, not only for the normal costs but also for any unforeseen calamities that might occur.

Size of the litter
The size of a litter of this breed can vary. Litters of seven puppies are not unusual, but neither are litters of just one or two. The average Jack Russell bitch will have four puppies.

The bitch

Just as not every bitch owner is cut out to be a breeder, not every bitch is cut out to be a mom. Her character should at least be typical of the breed, i.e. well balanced and people-friendly. She mustn't be nervous or display any other abnormal characteristics. Apart from these characteristics, that may be genetic, an unbalanced dam cannot set a good example for her puppies and the pups will copy a lot of their mother's behavior. She should also be a worthy representative of her breed.

A Parson being judged at a show.

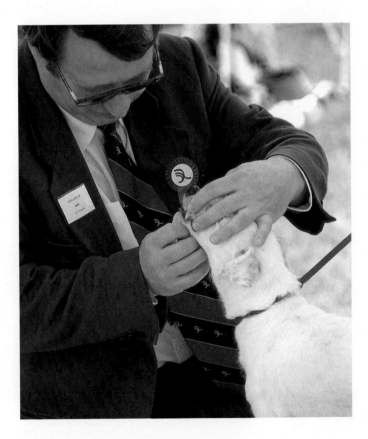

The best place to put this to the test is at a general dog show or a club match of the breeders' association. Sometimes a less attractive bitch can still make a valuable contribution to breeding. In that case, you should ask advice from an experienced breeder who knows your bitch's ancestry, and on this basis could suggest a dog that would form a good combination with her. This would be an impossible task for a beginner. Furthermore, the bitch should be in excellent condition. She should have no abnormalities or defects, of course, such as an allergy or loose kneecaps. Have her examined very thoroughly by a skilled vet. This is not something you have to do simply because you want to breed a good litter. Current legislation specifies that the breeder will be liable for the "damage" if the pups have any breed-related genetic abnormality or an abnormality not breed-related but which the bitch also has and of which the breeder was aware. An official prior examination, during which the bitch is declared free of any breed-related abnormalities could indemnify you against liability in a lawsuit. Unfortunately, more and more breeders are confronted with this kind of situation and more puppy buyers are choosing to take a case to court. A simple examination will not suffice. You need to be able to submit proof, in black and white, of her health status. Remember that a bitch that has herself been declared free of any afflictions, can still pass on (invisible) genetic defects from her parents and ancestors to her puppies. Pedigree research could clarify the situation. You should preferably seek the advice of an experienced breeder or the breeders' association.

The stud dog

Once your bitch has been approved in all respects, you can start to seek a suitable stud for her. In most cases, you can consult your own breeder because he or she will usually be familiar with the dogs at stud and know whether or not they would match your bitch's line. You can see the dogs in the flesh at club matches and general shows, or visit them at the breeders' homes. The association will usually be able to supply you with a list of addresses of stud dog owners. The dog should be of a

The dog should be at least as good as the bitch, preferably even better.

quality at least equal to that of your bitch, preferably even better. Whatever you do, don't use a dog with the same faults as your bitch, choose one that can compensate for her shortcomings. Even then, the saying that "breeding is a gamble" still holds true, since two excellent dogs could produce run-of-the-mill pups, just because the combination wasn't quite right. So always ask your bitch's breeder for his or her opinion and do the same with the owner of the stud dog.

The bitch should be perfectly fit before mating.

Season

Bitches are in season for a period of approximately three weeks every six months. The season starts with the swelling of the vulva and moderate loss of blood – the amount varies according to the individual bitch – that will decrease or stop altogether around the tenth day. The bitch is usually only fertile and willing to mate between days 10 and 14, although again there are exceptions. A bitch can be mated for the first time in her third or fourth season. Any sooner, and she will not have filled out enough and neither would she be mentally capable of fulfilling the hard task ahead of her. Waiting much longer won't help either, because of reduced fertility and a greater risk of complications. Well before mating, the bitch should be wormed with a broad-spectrum worming preparation and should be fully inoculated. She will, of course, be free of fleas, not overweight, and perfectly fit.

Mating

On the first day of her season you should contact the owner of the stud dog to make an appointment. It is common practice to have the bitch mated twice with one day's rest in between. Since the sperm stays active for 48 hours, this method bridges a period of four days, thus improving the chance of conception. During mating, the dog's penis swells, joining the genitals together, so to speak. This is known as "tying" and can last for ten minutes, for up to three quarters of an hour, or it may not even occur at all but, at any event, will not have any effect on whether the bitch conceives or not.

Bitches that are being mated for the first time can start to

Many bitches are nervous when mating for the first time.

panic during this "tying" and try to run off. This can be extremely painful for both dog and bitch, and can cause damage and infection. That is why many stud dog owners insist you keep your bitch leashed during mating.

Gestation

On average the gestation period (pregnancy) will last for 63 days from the first mating. During this period, you should ensure your bitch stays fit. Take her out walking several times a day to strengthen her muscles and make sure she doesn't hurt or strain herself, or get overexcited.

Throughout the gestation period you should not give her any extra vitamins, calcium, or food supplements, without first

A bitch toward the end of the gestation period.

consulting the vet. Anything you give her now, however innocent it may seem, can affect the unborn puppies. For the same reason, you should also be very careful about using anti-flea or worming preparations. For the first four weeks, you will notice little of your bitch's pregnancy, although she might behave a little strangely. She may be a little more subdued or more affectionate. From the fifth week, her abdomen will start to change shape and the mammary glands will start to swell. Around the sixth week, her belly will clearly be fatter, though if she is only carrying a small litter it might not grow very much at all. If you want to know for sure, you can have the vet examine her on the twenty-eighth day of gestation. That is the easiest time to feel the puppies or to see them on an ultrasonic scan.

Your bitch will not need any extra food at first, but you can start giving her a little to eat from about five weeks. Divide the meal into several portion, because the puppies put pressure on her stomach so that, understandably, she will not be able to digest as much food at once as she normally does. Her daily ration can gradually be doubled and, later, gradually reduced again once the pups have been weaned.

Requirements

- whelping-box
- overhead infrared heating lamp
- digital thermometer
- piles of clean towels
- a thick roll of thin corrugated cardboard
- puppy bottle and teats
- good bitch's milk substitute
- disinfectant
- accurate kitchen scales
- telephone number of vet
- notebook and pen
- dental floss
- scissors

The whelping-box

Whelping should preferably take place in a whelping-box, which will also serve as a "nest" for the mother and pups for a long while afterward. The whelping-box should be strong, easy to disinfect, and stand at least four inches off the ground, because both the dam and her pups are extremely sensitive to rising cold. Lay a sheet of thin corrugated cardboard, available from paper suppliers, on the bottom of the whelping-box. Corrugated cardboard gives the puppies something to grip when crawling in search of a teat, and no ink will rub off as it would from sheets of newspaper. Sheets and blankets are not safe, as the puppies could suffocate under them. Put the whelping-box in a quiet place on the ground floor of your home, that is not on a traffic route through the house and well away from any drafts.

An infrared lamp will generate extra warmth.

What your bitch initially needs more than anything else is rest. A lot of people coming and going, opening and closing doors, will particularly distress a first-time dam.

The ideal whelping-box should be around 24 x 30 inches in size and 8–12 inches high.

Signs that whelping is imminent

Although the average gestation period lasts for 63 days from the first mating, it is perfectly normal for a bitch to whelp a day or two earlier or later. A large litter will often be born a few days earlier and a small litter can keep everyone waiting for up to four or five days. Almost every bitch's body temperature will drop by a degree or so, about 24 hours before whelping begins. So take your bitch's temperature at the same time every day, starting about a week before she is due, so that you can tell when whelping has started.

Note that although this method works well for most bitches but there will always be exceptions. Behavioral changes will also often be a sign that whelping is imminent. Many bitches get quite restless a couple of days beforehand, some of them digging frantically in the whelping -box. You should stay alert at this stage, it wouldn't be the first time a bitch has dug herself a hole in the garden, and had her puppies there. Needless to say, the place she has chosen is often cold and damp and by no means the sterile environment you would wish, so it is not the ideal place for whelping. So don't let her out unsupervised for the time being.

Back-up

Every delivery is different and we cannot even start to consider all the possible complications and abnormalities that might arise within the scope of this book. Good contact with your bitch's breeder, the owner of the stud dog, or another experienced breeder you are otherwise well acquainted with, is therefore essential. These people can act as your telephone helpdesk during the tense hours or days ahead. Your veterinarian's attitude is equally important. If he or she has already made it clear that he or she is not inclined to make a house-call to assist you and your bitch in the middle of the night if need be, find a different vet with a more customer-oriented approach. If you are very unsure of yourself and your abilities as a canine midwife, perhaps a friend who is a fellow-breeder friend will be willing to come and help at home. Whatever the case, assistance from experienced people, even if only by telephone, is invaluable.

Labor

The bitch will have early contractions a few hours before the delivery. The actual delivery starts when the first strong, labor contractions come, and there will usually be no mistaking when that happens. Make a note of the time she has her first strong contraction, as under normal circumstances the first pup should be born within the next hour. If it takes longer, contact your vet immediately. The first thing to appear is usually the water sac or caul with the puppy inside it. As long as the water sac is not ruptured, the puppy will have no trouble breathing, so there is no need to worry if the sac temporarily disappears back into the vulva. When a puppy is born, the umbilical cord will often still be connected to the placenta. The placenta (or afterbirth) will usually follow shortly after the pup has been born, but can sometimes take a little longer. Always note the number of placentas that are delivered. If a placenta, or part of one, is left behind in the womb it can make the dam (fatally) ill. An experienced bitch will bite through the water sac and the umbilical cord. She will lick her puppy clean, stimulating it to breathe. An inexperienced dam may need

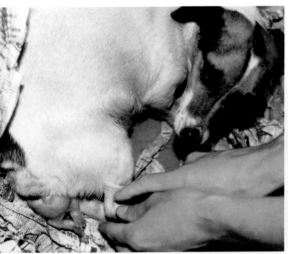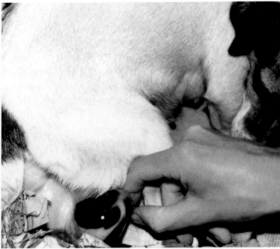

Left:
A double compli-
cation: a breech
position and an
upside-down
delivery.

help from you. Remove the water sac, starting at the mouth so that the puppy does not get fluid in its lungs when it takes its first breaths. Tie dental floss around the umbilical cord, about an inch from the pup's body and cut the cord on the placenta side. Bitches usually eat the placentas; this is perfectly natural and is apparently good for the milk supply. However, if there are more than five pups, remove the other placentas. The next puppy could be born quickly, but could take half an hour or more.

Right:
Open the sac
near the mouth
first, so the pup
can breath.

Immediately after labor

Once the last pup has been born, the dam will become calmer and will often sleep. Give her some water to drink and take her into the garden so that she can relieve herself. In the

What mother and
pup need most of
all is rest.

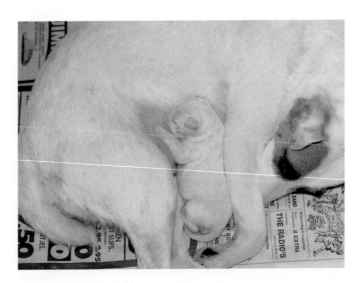

meantime, someone else can weigh the puppies and clean the whelping box.

The infrared lamp should be switched on 24 hours a day. It should be hung over the whelping box, 8-12 inches above the dam's shoulders. This is particularly important in winter, but will not usually be necessary in summer. Note the different features, sex, and weight of each puppy. Weigh the pups at the same time each day and record their weights in a table. This will enable you to keep a close eye on the individual growth of each puppy and enable you to intervene (in time) if growth stagnates or falls short of the rest of the litter. Always ask the veterinarian to visit shortly after the delivery, to examine the puppies and dam. He will usually give the dam an injection to make the womb contract. If there a placenta or any part of it is left in the womb, this will expel it. You could also ask your vet to bring some worming preparations, so that you have them ready. Do not be persuaded to take the dam and her pups to the practice. The risk of infection is far too great to go dragging them around, and it would all be unnecessarily stressful for the bitch. It just makes life easier for the vet. What the dam and her puppies need more than anything else for the first two weeks, is as much rest as possible.

The average weight at birth is 6–7 ounces.

The first weeks

You will notice that the bitch will have a discharge for the first couple of weeks after the birth of her pups. The discharge will be red first, later becoming light pink. Take the bitch's temperature every day and contact your vet if the temperature rises or falls more than one degree. A dog's normal body temperature varies between 99.5°F and 101.3°F. You should also consult your vet if the mammary glands change color or harden. You will make life a little less uncomfortable for the dam, and relieve her sensitive mammary glands, if you cut or file the puppies' sharp nails once a week. If the litter and the dam are all healthy, they will not create much work for you in the first few weeks. In countries in which tail-docking is allowed, the tails are docked between the second and fourth day after the pups are born. The dam cares for her offspring, feeds them, massages their bellies, and cleans up after them. Satisfied, healthy puppies sleep a lot and you will hardly hear a squeak from them. If they are not getting enough milk, if they are cold, or something else is wrong, you will notice it in their behavior straight away. They will crawl around the whelping-box, yapping and squeaking, or lie softly moaning in a corner.

Three satisfied, three-day old puppies, sound asleep.

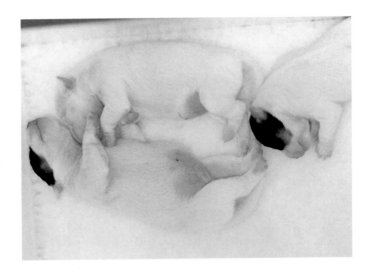

A three-week old litter.

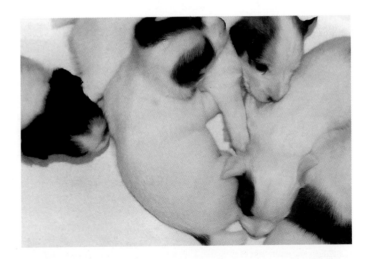

Always contact your vet immediately if this happens because the puppies are still very vulnerable. Leaving them for even half a day longer could be fatal. Puppies don't stay as small and helpless as this forever; their eyes open around day 10 and by the time they are two-and-a-half to three weeks old they will be taking their first wobbly steps.

3–6 weeks

Although some antibodies are provided in the mother's milk, the puppies are still very susceptible to disease at this early stage, so do not allow any strange dogs near them and don't take the dam out onto the street yet. From anywhere between

Eight weeks old and big enough to go to their new owners.

Two rough-haired Parson Jack Russell terriers.

pies all the time, give her a chance to get away from them for a while if she clearly wants to do so. Take the puppies with you when you go out, avoiding places that many other dogs frequent, because until they have had their second inoculation they are not sufficiently protected against disease. If you have completed all the application forms correctly, you can expect someone from the pedigree association to come and fit the puppies with chips. When the puppies are eight weeks old, this is the ideal age for them to go to their new homes.

IMPORTANT ADDRESSES

Jack Russell Terrier Association of America
Maria Sacco, President
PO Box 4541
Danbury, CT 06813
jrtaa_02@yahoo.com
Nancy Dougherty, Secretary
P.O. Box 121
Lewisville, PA 19351
Ndoughe982@aol.com

JRTTC Canada
Doris Oram, President
Box 126
Tugaskee, SK.,
S0H 4B0
Tel: (306)-796-4755
fax: (306)-759-2212
Email: doris@jrtcc.com

Bobbi Deline – Vice President /Secretary
723 Concession 7, RR #4
Niagara-on-the-Lake, Ontario
L0S 1J0
Tel: (905)-684-9841
Email: bobbi@jrtcc.com

Wendy Schmaltz – Rescue/Reps/Affiliates Committee
Box 56
Beiseker, Alberta
T0M 0G0,
Tel: (403) 935 4543
Email: wendy@jrtcc.comL0R 2H5
Tel: (905)-690-4247

ACKNOWLEDGEMENTS AND PHOTO CREDITS

The author and publisher wish to thank everyone who contributed photographs to this book, especially John Roskam, Jan Dekker, Susanne Stabel, Karin Jenniskens, and Jan Hoedemakers, who together own most of the dogs photographed. We would also like to thank the firms of Van Riel Distripet in Waalwijk, Dynabone in Kruisland, and Break The Chain in IJmuiden, for submitting photographs of the products shown in this book.

Thanks also to Jan Dekker, whose valuable notes on the manuscript have been incorporated into this edition.

All photographs by Esther Verhoef, with the exception of:

Karin Jenniskens, pages: 11, 14, 31, 32, 33, 35, 40, 104, 105, 118, 122, 123 (top), 124 (bottom), 125 (top).
Susanne Stabel, page 38.
Jos van Dooren, page 94.
Jos Roskam and Jan Dekker, pages: 120, 123 (bottom), 124 (top).

The black-and-white photographs and drawings were taken from *Hondenrassen* (published by Van Bylandt).